fast foods

quadrille

This edition first published in 2007 by **Quadrille Publishing Limited**
Alhambra House, 27-31 Charing Cross Road, London WC2H 0LS

Editorial Director Jane O'Shea
Creative Director Helen Lewis
Editor Kathy Steer
Designer Katherine Case
Production Bridget Fish

Text © 2007 Seven Publishing Group
Photography © 2007 Seven Publishing Group
(for a full list of contributors and photographers, see pages 284–5)
Design and layout © 2007 Quadrille Publishing Limited

Most of the material in this volume was previously published in **delicious**.
magazine or **Sainsbury's Magazine** and was provided courtesy of the Seven
Publishing Group.

Cataloguing in Publication Data:
a catalogue record for this book is available from the British Library.

ISBN 978 184400 486 7
Printed in China

Cookery notes
All spoon measures are level unless otherwise stated: 1 teaspoon = 5 ml
spoon; 1 tablespoon = 15 ml spoon.Use fresh herbs unless dried herbs are
suggested. Use sea salt and freshly ground black pepper unless otherwise
stated. Free-range eggs are recommended and large eggs should be used
except where a different size is specified. Recipes which feature raw or
lightly cooked eggs should be avoided by anyone who is pregnant or in a
vulnerable health group.

Contents

6 introduction

8 **fast** snacks, soups & starters

52 **fast** meat & poultry

104 **fast** fish & shellfish

146 **fast** pasta, gnocchi, rice & noodles

202 **fast** vegetables, pulses & eggs

246 **fast** puddings

284 acknowledgements

286 index

Introduction

The majority of the recipes in this collection are ready in under half an hour and many can be on the table in just a few minutes. But cooking quickly doesn't mean missing out on depths of flavour, or sacrificing taste and quality. What it does mean is less time in the kitchen, and more time to do everything else. It is absolutely possible to create, in a matter of minutes rather than hours, wholesome, delicious meals to delight the taste buds and dishes to inspire and impress.

Chapters are grouped around the main ingredient for easy selection, and you'll find diverse global dishes wonderfully represented. The recipes range from richly creamed Thai curries with fragrant lemongrass and chilli, to honeyed duck stir-fries, typical of regional Chinese cooking, to the citrus flavours and warm spices of North Africa and on through to the sun-ripened tomatoes and olives of the Mediterranean.

These are not shortcut recipes that rely on pre-prepared components, they are dishes that can be made quickly using fresh, good quality, healthy ingredients. With easy-to-follow instructions, as well as clever tips and suggestions for adapting the basic dishes, you will never need to pick up a take-away Chinese or micro-wave chilli again when you could be making the real thing.

fast snacks, soups & starters

Chicken & aubergine melts

Serves 4

2 skinless chicken breasts, each
about 150g

2 tbsp olive oil, plus extra for
brushing

1 small aubergine, cut into 1cm
slices

1 ciabatta loaf, halved lengthways

90g ready-made aïoli

handful of rocket leaves

salt and pepper

150g mozzarella cheese, sliced

1 Heat a griddle pan. Slice the chicken breasts in half horizontally and
rub with olive oil. Griddle for 5–7 minutes on each side, then rest on a plate.
2 Brush the aubergine slices with olive oil and griddle on each side
for 2 minutes and set aside.
3 Preheat the grill. Drizzle 2 tbsp olive oil over both cut sides of the ciabatta
and grill until golden.
4 Spread the aïoli on one half and top with rocket. Lay the aubergine and
chicken on top, season and drizzle over any chicken juices. Add the
mozzarella and grill until the cheese melts. Top with the remaining ciabatta
half and cut into four portions.

Chorizo, roasted pepper & rocket sandwich

Serves 2
110g chorizo de pueblo
2 ciabatta buns, halved
225g bottled roasted red peppers
100g rocket leaves
1 tbsp extra virgin olive oil
salt and pepper

1 Preheat a ridged griddle pan or barbecue. Cut the chorizo in half lengthways and remove the outer casing.
2 Toast the cut sides of the ciabatta on the griddle pan or barbecue, then remove and keep warm.
3 Cook the chorizo on the griddle pan or barbecue until crisp on both sides.
4 Fill the toasted buns with the roasted peppers, chargrilled chorizo and a handful of rocket, drizzle with a little extra virgin olive oil, season and eat while still hot.

Red pepper & goats' cheese toasted panini

Serves 1

1 panini roll
2 tbsp low-fat mayonnaise
3 pieces roasted red pepper from a
    jar (about 25g), dried on kitchen
    paper
50g soft goats' cheese, cut into slices
freshly ground black pepper
few lettuce leaves

1 Preheat the grill to medium. Halve the panini and toast both sides under the hot grill. Spread the cut sides with mayonnaise.
2 Arrange the pepper pieces on top of the mayonnaise-coated base. Top with goats' cheese slices and season with pepper. Add a few small lettuce leaves and sandwich together with the top of the panini.

You will find red peppers, ready roasted and sold in jars, at most supermarkets – they taste sweet and tender and are a great option for vegetarians. Once the jar is open, keep in the fridge and use within a week.

Sausage pittas with caramelised onions

Serves 6
200ml mayonnaise
2 tbsp wholegrain mustard
large pinch of cayenne pepper
salt and pepper
12 good quality pork and herb
  sausages

6 flatbreads, pitta breads or flour
  tortillas
small bag rocket leaves
350g jar caramelised onion chutney
  or other mild chutney, to serve

1 Mix the mayonnaise, mustard and cayenne pepper together, then season to taste and set aside.
2 Light the barbecue, following the manufacturer's instructions. Cook the sausages on the hot barbecue for 10–12 minutes, turning two or three times until cooked through.
3 Lightly barbecue the breads for about 30 seconds each side. Top with some rocket, two hot sausages, caramelised onion chutney and a good dollop of the mustard mayonnaise to finish.

You can also cook the sausages in the oven at 200°C/fan oven 180°C/Gas 6 for about 25–30 minutes. Warm the flatbreads in a pan for 30 seconds on each side.

Mozzarella, figs & Parma ham bruschetta

Serves 2
150g mozzarella cheese
4 ripe figs, quartered
3 vine-ripened tomatoes, quartered
50g rocket leaves
85g Parma ham
2 thick slices country-style bread,
  toasted

salt and pepper
aged balsamic vinegar, for drizzling
extra virgin olive oil, for drizzling
20g fresh basil, leaves only, roughly
  torn

1 Tear up the mozzarella into bite-sized pieces.
2 Arrange the figs, mozzarella pieces, tomatoes and rocket on top of the toasted bread.
3 Drape over the Parma ham. Season and drizzle with the balsamic vinegar and olive oil. Scatter over the basil and serve.

Roquefort or Dolcelatte would also make ideal alternatives for the mozzarella.

Smart beans on toast

Serves 2

175g chorizo sausage (skin
   removed), halved and cut into
   1cm slices
1 small red onion, sliced
1 red pepper, seeded and cut into
   1cm cubes
pinch of dried chilli flakes

1 tsp fennel seeds
410g can butter beans in water,
   drained and rinsed
400g can chopped tomatoes
150ml water
salt and pepper
2 thick slices ciabatta
1 tbsp extra virgin olive oil

1 Heat a non-stick deep-sided frying pan, add the chorizo slices, onion, red pepper, chilli flakes and fennel seeds. Cook gently for 10 minutes, stirring the vegetables into the chorizo juices.

2 Add the butter beans, tomatoes and the water, then season with salt and pepper and stir together. Simmer for 10–15 minutes or until the red pepper is tender and the beans have softened slightly.

3 Meanwhile, toast the ciabatta and drizzle with the olive oil. Spoon the chorizo and bean mixture over the toasted ciabatta and serve.

If you have a can of cannellini beans in your storecupboard, they are a good substitute for butter beans.

Parma ham & smoked mozzarella pizza

Illustrated on the following pages

Makes 32

2 fresh thin and crispy pizza bases
  (330g packet)
250g ready-made tomato and herb
  pizza topping
150g smoked mozzarella cheese,
  finely diced

6 slices Parma ham, torn into strips
salt and pepper
30g wild rocket leaves
extra virgin olive oil, for drizzling

1 Preheat the oven to 220°C/fan oven 200°C/Gas 7. Place each pizza base on a non-stick baking sheet. Spread over the topping, going as close to the edge as you can. Dot with mozzarella and Parma ham and season lightly. Bake for 12–15 minutes until the base is golden and the topping is hot.
2 Top each pizza with a few rocket leaves, then drizzle with a little olive oil. Cut each into 16 thin wedges. Transfer to serving plates and serve hot or at room temperature.

Tomato, sausage & Emmental croissants

Serves 4

4 thick, plump sausages of your choice
2 tbsp olive oil
12 baby plum or cherry tomatoes
pinch of dried chilli flakes

2 tbsp crème fraîche
4 fresh all-butter croissants
100g Emmental cheese, coarsely grated
fresh flat leaf parsley, torn, to garnish

1 Preheat the oven to 200°C/fan oven 180°C/Gas 6. Split the skin on the sausages and squeeze out the meat. Discard the skins.

2 Heat the oil in a frying pan and crumble in the sausagemeat. Cook for 4–5 minutes, stirring occasionally until browned and slightly crisp in places. Cut the tomatoes in half and add to the pan. Cook for 3–4 minutes, stirring occasionally until the tomatoes are wilted. Add the chilli flakes and stir for 1 minute. Add the crème fraîche and cook for 1–2 minutes until thickened.

3 Make a split down the centre of each croissant. Stir 75g of the Emmental into the sausage mixture, then divide between the croissants. Put on a baking tray and sprinkle the remaining cheese over the top. Bake for 5 minutes until they are hot and the cheese has melted. Garnish with torn parsley. Serve hot or warm.

Pea, lettuce & tarragon soup

Serves 4
40g butter
6 spring onions, sliced
675g freshly shelled or frozen peas
leaves from 4 fresh tarragon sprigs
225g romaine lettuce, finely
  shredded

1 litre hot fresh vegetable stock
salt and pepper
2 tbsp crème fraîche
watercress sprigs, to garnish
  (optional)

1 Melt the butter in a large saucepan over a medium heat. Add the spring onions and cook, stirring, for 2 minutes. Stir in three-quarters of the peas, half the tarragon and all the lettuce. Cook for 1 minute.
2 Add the hot stock, bring to the boil, cover and simmer for 8–10 minutes if the peas are fresh, 5 minutes if frozen, or until tender.
3 Whiz the soup in a blender with the remaining tarragon, until smooth. Pass through a fine sieve into a clean saucepan. Stir in the rest of the peas and allow to simmer gently for 4–5 minutes until the peas are just tender. Season to taste.
4 Divide the soup between bowls, swirl the crème fraîche into each and garnish with watercress sprigs, if you like.

Tuscan bean soup with rosemary & pesto

Serves 3–4

2 tbsp olive oil, plus extra for
   drizzling
1 large onion, sliced
1 fat garlic clove, chopped
4 fresh rosemary sprigs, leaves only
2 x 410g cans cannellini beans,
   drained and rinsed

400g can chopped tomatoes with
   herbs
275ml hot vegetable stock
salt and pepper
150g ready-made fresh green pesto

1 Heat the 2 tbsp olive oil in a medium saucepan. Add the sliced onion, chopped garlic and rosemary leaves and cook over a medium heat for 8 minutes or until the onion has softened.

2 Add half the cannellini beans to the saucepan with the chopped tomatoes. Stir together, then whiz in a blender until smooth.

3 Return the soup to the pan, add the stock and the rest of the beans. Heat until piping hot, then season.

4 Serve in bowls, drizzle with a little olive oil and top with a generous dollop of pesto.

Serve with plenty of hot ciabatta bread and some Italian cheeses as a warming soup for a cold winter's night.

Chilled avocado soup with zingy salsa

Serves 4 for lunch or 6 as a starter
2 ripe avocados
juice of 1½ limes
1 cucumber, peeled, seeded and
   roughly chopped
2 spring onions, chopped
small handful of fresh coriander,
   stalks and leaves separated
handful of ice cubes, roughly
   crushed
400ml chilled vegetable stock
200g Greek yogurt

few dashes of Tabasco sauce
salt and pepper
extra virgin olive oil, to serve

For the salsa
4 ripe plum tomatoes, seeded and
   diced
2 spring onions, finely chopped
few dashes of Tabasco sauce
small handful of chopped fresh
   coriander
juice of ½ lime

1 Make the salsa by mixing all the ingredients together in a bowl. Season, cover and chill until needed.
2 Make the soup. Halve and stone the avocados, scoop out the flesh with a spoon and put into a food processor. Add the lime juice, chopped cucumber, chopped spring onions, coriander stalks, ice and half the vegetable stock and whiz until smooth. Tip into a large bowl and stir in the rest of the stock, yogurt and Tabasco sauce. Chop the coriander leaves, stir into the soup and season to taste.
3 Divide the soup between four or six bowls and top each one with a spoonful of salsa and a drizzle of olive oil.

Make the salsa the day before and keep it covered in the fridge until you're ready to eat. The soup can also be frozen for up to a month, then defrost at room temperature, stir until smooth and serve chilled.

Grilled crottin wrapped in prosciutto

Serves 1
100g crottin (French goats' cheese)
1 slice prosciutto
1 ciabatta loaf, sliced and toasted
1 tbsp olive oil, for drizzling
25g black olives, mashed
100g sprig slow-roasted cherry
   tomatoes on the vine, to serve

1 Preheat the grill to medium. Wrap a crottin in a paper-thin slice of
prosciutto and grill for about 5 minutes, turning once.
2 Set on a slice of toasted ciabatta rubbed with oil and thinly spread with
mashed black olives. Serve with the slow-roasted cherry tomatoes.

To cook the slow-roasted tomatoes, preheat the
oven to 200°C/fan oven 180°C/Gas 6. Toss the
sprig of cherry tomatoes in a little olive oil
and roast for 4–5 minutes.

Tomato & goats' cheese tarts

Serves 4
375g ready-rolled puff pastry
plain flour, for dusting
150g goats' cheese
250g vine cherry or pomodorino
  tomatoes, halved
salt and pepper
1 egg, beaten with a little water

To finish
extra virgin olive oil, for drizzling
4 large fresh basil sprigs
handful of rocket leaves
4 slices Parma ham (optional)

1 Preheat the oven to 200°C/fan oven 180°C/Gas 6. Lay the pastry on a surface lightly dusted with flour. Trim off the edges to neaten and cut the pastry to make four equal-size squares. Put on a baking tray and chill until the filling is ready.
2 Break the cheese into craggy pieces. Arrange the tomato halves and goats' cheese in the centre of each pastry square. Don't worry if the piles look quite high, the pastry will cook up around them. Season well, then brush the edges with the beaten egg wash and bake in the oven for 15–18 minutes until puffed and golden.
3 Serve as they are, hot from the oven, drizzled with a little olive oil and garnished with a large basil sprig and some rocket. Alternatively, top each tart with a slice of Parma ham before garnishing with the basil and rocket.

Runner bean salad with feta cheese

Serves 4

700g runner beans, sliced
salt and pepper
250g ripe tomatoes, cut into chunks
½ red onion, finely chopped
2 tbsp red wine vinegar

4 tbsp olive oil
2 tbsp chopped fresh herbs, such as
   basil and parsley
200g Feta cheese, crumbled
3 tbsp pitted Kalamata olives,
   chopped

1 Cook the runner beans in a saucepan of boiling salted water for
5–6 minutes or until tender. Leave to cool.

2 When the beans are cool, combine with the tomatoes and onion in a large
serving bowl.

3 Whisk the vinegar, oil and herbs together in another bowl and season
generously with salt and pepper. Toss with the beans and tomatoes. Sprinkle
over the crumbled Feta and chopped olives and serve.

Summery Spanish-style soup

Illustrated on the following pages

Serves 4

1 tbsp olive oil
1 onion, chopped
2 carrots, sliced
400g can chopped tomatoes
1.5 litres hot vegetable stock
410g can mixed pulses, drained
   and rinsed

75g small soup pasta shapes
2 Savoy cabbage leaves, shredded
salt and pepper
handful of flat leaf parsley, roughly
   chopped
freshly grated Parmesan cheese,
   to serve

1 Heat the oil in a large saucepan. Add the onion and carrot and cook for
5 minutes. Add the chopped tomato, hot stock and pulses, bring to the boil,
then reduce the heat and simmer for 5 minutes.
2 Stir in the pasta shapes and simmer for 5 minutes. Add the cabbage,
season and cook for a further 2–3 minutes until the pasta is just cooked.
3 Stir in the parsley and divide between four warmed soup bowls. Serve with
grated Parmesan and chunks of crusty bread, if you like.

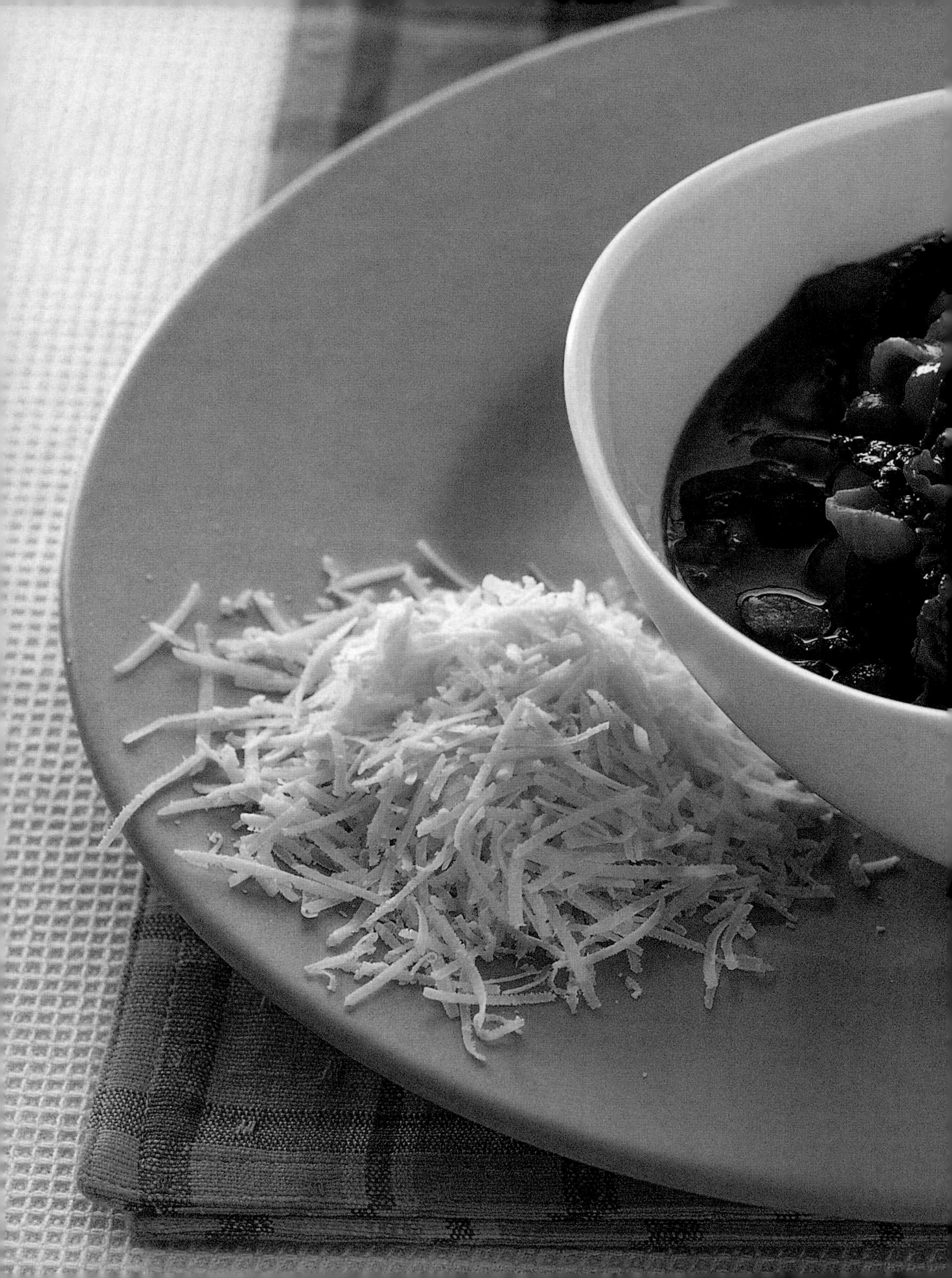

Egg with mustard mayo & cress

Serves 2
2–3 organic eggs
20g salad cress
pinch of paprika (optional)

For the mayo
1 organic egg
1–2 tsp Dijon mustard
salt and white pepper
200ml groundnut or grapeseed oil
1–2 tbsp mild olive oil
1–2 tsp tarragon white wine vinegar

1 To make the mayo, place the egg, ½ tsp mustard and a pinch of salt in a food processor and start the motor. Add the groundnut oil through the funnel in a thin, steady stream. Stop the motor frequently to scrape down the sides of the bowl. When all the oil is added, the mayo should be light in colour and texture and thick like whipped butter. Whisk in the olive oil and additional mustard to taste, then whisk in vinegar to taste. Season with more salt, if necessary and pepper.
2 To cook the eggs, place them in a small saucepan and cover with cold water. Bring to a gentle simmer then cook for 5–6 minutes. Plunge the eggs immediately into a bowl of cold water then tap the shell on the side of the bowl to crack it and leave in the cold water for at least 5 minutes to cool.
3 Shell the eggs and either slice or cut in half and arrange on two plates. Spoon some mayo over the egg, then scatter over the cress. Add a sprinkle of paprika, if you like, and serve with buttered wholemeal soda bread.

If you prefer a thicker mayonnaise, you will need two egg yolks rather than a whole egg and maybe a little more oil. Scatter over 100g cooked and shelled large prawns before serving for a more substantial dish.

Toasted muffins with smoked salmon

Serves 2
4 medium eggs
5 tbsp crème fraîche
1 tbsp finely chopped fresh chives
salt and pepper

2 muffins
a little butter
3 handfuls of young-leaf spinach
125g smoked salmon

1 Pour 2.5cm of boiling water into a small frying pan and bring back to a very gentle simmer. Gently break the eggs into the water, leave for 1 minute and then take off the heat. Leave for 10 minutes.

2 Meanwhile, warm the crème fraîche in a pan over a low heat. Stir in the chives and a good grinding of pepper. Split the muffins in half and toast them. Butter each half, then top with a few spinach leaves and the smoked salmon.

3 Using a slotted spoon, lift the eggs out of the water and place on top of the smoked salmon, pour over half the crème fraîche and chopped chives. Toss the remaining spinach with the remaining crème fraîche and chives. Serve with the muffins.

This is a quick version of eggs Benedict, which uses up any smoked salmon you might have left. Smoked trout would also work well.

Spiced & buttered crab

Illustrated on the following pages

Serves 7
2 hard-boiled eggs, finely chopped
400g fresh white crabmeat
2 tbsp mayonnaise
40g butter, melted
1 tsp cayenne pepper, plus extra to
  sprinkle

large pinch of ground allspice
salt and pepper
1 pink shallot, thinly sliced
small handful of fresh basil leaves

1 Put the eggs, crabmeat, mayonnaise, butter and spices into a bowl. Mix and season to taste. Divide between six small bowls or ramekins and chill until ready to serve.
2 Top each serving with a few slices of shallot, some fresh basil and a sprinkling of cayenne pepper. Serve with warm French bread or toast.

You can make this the day before, then cover and chill overnight. Bring back to room temperature before serving. If you can't get fresh white crabmeat, buy frozen and thaw it overnight in the fridge. Drain off the excess liquid before using.

Chicken, pasta & butter bean ramen

Serves 2

600ml hot chicken stock
2 skinless chicken breasts, sliced
75g dried spaghetti, broken into
   short lengths
410g can butter beans, drained and
   rinsed
125g cherry tomatoes, halved
1 red chilli, seeded and finely sliced
salt and pepper
handful of chopped fresh parsley

1 Pour the stock into a large saucepan and bring to the boil over a medium heat, then add the sliced chicken and spaghetti and simmer, partially covered, for 5 minutes.

2 Stir in the butter beans, halved cherry tomatoes and finely sliced red chilli and cook for 2–3 minutes until the chicken and spaghetti are cooked.

3 Season and stir in a handful of chopped fresh parsley. Divide between deep bowls and serve with crusty bread.

Mussels in a coconut & lemon grass broth

Serves 4

2kg fresh mussels, in their shells
1 tsp cumin seeds
4 lemon grass stalks, outer layers
    discarded, cores bashed and finely
    chopped
1 tbsp chopped fresh root ginger
2 red chillies, seeded and chopped
2 garlic cloves, chopped

1 tbsp sunflower oil
400ml can coconut milk
1 tbsp Thai fish sauce
finely grated zest and juice of 1 lime
6 tbsp chopped fresh coriander

To finish
coriander sprigs
lime wedges

1 Scrub the mussels well, removing the beards and any barnacles. Discard any with broken shells or any that don't close tight when tapped on a hard surface.
2 Lightly crush the cumin seeds with a pestle and mortar, then add the lemon grass, ginger, chillies and garlic and bash to a paste.
3 Heat the oil in a very large pan – ideally, a wok. Add the spice paste and gently cook for 1 minute, then add the coconut milk and bring to the boil. Tip in the mussels, then cover and cook, shaking the pan every now and then, for about 3 minutes or until all the mussels have opened. Discard any that remain shut.
4 Add the fish sauce, lime zest and juice and chopped coriander. Ladle into warmed bowls, garnish with coriander sprigs and serve with lime wedges.

You don't need much more than a squeeze of lime to enjoy this quick lunch. If you want to turn it into a big supper, serve with hot, sticky rice.

fast
meat &
poultry

Cajun beef wraps

Serves 4

1 heaped tsp Cajun seasoning
4 tsp olive oil
225g sirloin steak, trimmed of all fat
1 large red onion, cut into 8 wedges
4 tortilla wraps

4 tbsp lime juice
100g ready-made red pepper
  houmous
2 large carrots, grated
100g salad leaves

1 Preheat the grill to its highest setting.
2 Meanwhile, mix the Cajun seasoning and oil together in a small bowl and spread over both sides of the steak. Place on a small baking tray and scatter the onion around the outside. Grill the steak for 3–4 minutes, then turn over and toss the onion in the juices before grilling again for 3–4 minutes or until cooked to your liking. Be careful that the onions don't burn. Remove from the grill and transfer the steak to a board.
3 Heat the wraps according to the packet instructions, then add the lime juice to the houmous and spread half over the wraps. Scatter with grated carrot and salad leaves. Thinly slice the steak and divide it and the onion between the wraps. Fold over or roll up and serve.

Cheat's beef stroganoff

Serves 4
225g long-grain rice
500g quick-frying beef steaks, cut
  into thin strips
1 tsp mixed peppercorns, crushed
1 tbsp olive oil
1 onion, finely sliced

150g closed cup mushrooms, wiped
  and halved
3 tbsp water
284ml carton soured cream
2 tsp paprika
pepper

1 Cook the rice according to the packet instructions. Meanwhile, put the beef strips into a shallow dish, add the crushed peppercorns and toss to coat. Set aside.

2 Heat the oil in a large frying pan over a medium heat. Add the onion and cook for 3–4 minutes or until soft but not coloured.

3 Add the mushrooms and cook for a further 5 minutes. Increase the heat, add the beef strips and fry for 4–5 minutes or until the juices have evaporated and the meat is brown. Add the water and let bubble to deglaze the pan.

4 Stir in most of the soured cream and half the paprika, and gently heat until warmed through. Check the seasoning.

5 Spoon the beef stroganoff onto serving plates. Top with the remaining soured cream, season with the remaining paprika and black pepper and serve with the rice.

For an even cheaper version, use pork loin steaks. Bulk-buying keeps costs down and you can always freeze what you don't need.

Peppered steak with a rich shallot sauce

Serves 4
For the sauce
50g butter
4 shallots, finely sliced
4 tbsp Cognac
200ml red wine
200ml hot beef stock
salt and pepper

For the steaks
olive oil, for brushing
2 tbsp crushed black peppercorns
4 rump or sirloin steaks

1 To make the sauce, melt 25g butter in a large frying pan over a medium heat. Add the sliced shallots and cook for 2–3 minutes to soften. Pour in the Cognac, boil for 1 minute, then add the red wine. Increase the heat and boil for a few minutes to reduce by half.

2 Pour in the hot beef stock and boil until reduced by half again. Stir in the remaining 25g butter, season to taste and leave over a low heat.

3 Meanwhile, brush a griddle or frying pan with a little oil and place over a high heat. Press the crushed black peppercorns all over the steaks. Place in the hot pan and cook for 2–5 minutes each side, depending how you like them cooked.

4 Remove the steaks from the pan and set aside for 2 minutes to rest. Divide between four serving plates, pour over the sauce and serve with thinly cut oven chips and grilled vine tomatoes.

Make up the hot beef stock from ½ stock cube.

Beef steak chilli con carne

Serves 2

2 tbsp vegetable oil
½ tsp hot paprika
1 tsp ground cumin
2 large beef frying steaks, each about 200g, sliced

salt and pepper
215g can kidney beans, drained and rinsed
2 ripe tomatoes, roughly diced
15g chopped fresh coriander, plus extra sprigs to garnish

1 Mix the oil, hot paprika and ground cumin together in a medium bowl. Add the sliced beef, season with salt and pepper and mix well. Set aside for 10 minutes to marinate.

2 Heat a large frying pan over a medium heat. Add the marinated beef and stir-fry for 1–2 minutes until browned. Stir in the kidney beans, roughly diced tomatoes and a splash of water. Simmer for 5 minutes until the tomatoes are softened.

3 Stir in some chopped fresh coriander, divide between four plates and top each with a coriander sprig. Serve with boiled basmati rice and a spoonful of ready-made guacamole.

Stir-fried kale with beef & black bean sauce

Serves 4

1½ level tbsp cornflour
2 tbsp oyster sauce
2 tbsp dark soy sauce
pepper
700g rump steak, trimmed and cut
    into strips
1½ tbsp groundnut or other
    flavourless oil, plus extra if needed
250g curly kale, tough stalks
    trimmed and roughly shredded
250ml vegetable stock
2 tbsp black bean sauce

1 Put the cornflour, oyster sauce, soy sauce and pepper into a bowl and mix well. Add the steak and stir to coat.
2 Heat the oil in a wok or frying pan until very hot. Keeping the heat high, add half of the steak and leave to brown, then turn. Remove from the heat, strain through a sieve to get rid of most of the fat, then repeat with the second batch, adding more oil if necessary. Set aside in a warm place.
3 Wipe the pan, add the kale and stir-fry for 2 minutes. Add the stock and cook, uncovered, turning occasionally, until the kale is tender and the stock has been absorbed. Add the black bean sauce and beef. Toss together and serve immediately with boiled rice or noodles.

Pork, pesto & mozzarella parcels

Illustrated on the following pages

Serves 2

2 outdoor-reared pork escalopes
2–3 tbsp spinach and Parmesan or
   basil pesto
150g mozzarella cheese, cut into
   4 slices
salt and pepper
3 tbsp olive oil

75ml white wine
400g can cannellini beans, drained
   and rinsed
1 large garlic clove, crushed
juice of ½ lemon
1 rounded tbsp fresh parsley,
   chopped
rocket leaves, to serve (optional)

1 Bash the escalopes with a rolling pin until halved in thickness. Cut each one in half widthways and spread with the pesto. Lay a slice of mozzarella on each one, season with pepper and roll up. Secure with a cocktail stick.
2 Heat half the oil in a frying pan and brown the parcels, then fry over a medium heat for 6–8 minutes, turning once. Pour away the excess oil. Add the wine and let bubble for 3 minutes.
3 Meanwhile, heat the beans with the remaining oil, the garlic, lemon juice, parsley and seasoning in a separate pan. Spoon on to plates, top with the parcels and pour over the pan juices. Remove the cocktail sticks and serve with the rocket leaves, if you like.

Gammon steaks with mustard & cider sauce

Serves 4
4 gammon steaks, each about 150g
200ml cider
2 tbsp grainy mustard
200ml crème fraîche
pepper

1 Heat a large frying pan and, when hot, fry the gammon steaks for
3–5 minutes on each side. You will need to do this in 2 batches. Remove
from the pan as they are ready and keep warm in a low oven.
2 Add the cider to the pan, bring to the boil and simmer for 2 minutes. Stir
in the mustard. Remove from the heat and mix in the crème fraîche. Season
with pepper and serve with steamed greens and ready-made mashed potato.

Pork fillet with mushrooms & beans

Serves 2

400g pork fillet, trimmed and cut in
  half widthways
1 large garlic clove, sliced
3 tbsp olive oil
2 pinches of crushed chilli flakes
2 tbsp sherry vinegar
salt and pepper
250g flat mushrooms, thickly sliced
400g can flageolet beans, rinsed and
  drained
2 tbsp fresh parsley sprigs, leaves
  removed and chopped, plus a few
  small sprigs reserved to garnish

1 Preheat the oven to 220°C/fan oven 200°C/Gas 7. Meanwhile, make small cuts in the pork and stud with the garlic slices. Put into a roasting tin, rub with 1½ tbsp oil, the chilli flakes and half the sherry vinegar. Season with salt and pepper and roast for 10 minutes.

2 Remove from the oven, turn over and add the mushrooms, beans, the remaining oil and sherry vinegar. Toss together and roast for a further 10–15 minutes.

3 Transfer the pork to a board to rest for 5 minutes before slicing. Toss the chopped parsley into the bean mixture and serve with the pork. Scatter with the reserved parsley sprigs.

This one-tray dish can be served with a simple green salad.

Pork with spinach, raisins & pine nuts

Serves 2
2 x 150g boneless loin pork steaks
salt and pepper
300g spinach leaves, rinsed and
    drained

1 tbsp olive oil
1½ tbsp raisins
2 tbsp pine nuts
4 tbsp Spanish sherry vinegar

1 Preheat the grill to its highest setting. Season the pork, then grill the steaks on a baking tray for 20 minutes, turning them halfway through.
2 Meanwhile, put the spinach into a large saucepan and wilt over a medium heat, about 2 minutes. Tip the spinach into a colander and press well with a saucer to extract all the excess moisture.
3 Heat the oil in the saucepan. Add the raisins and pine nuts and toss together over a high heat for a couple of minutes or until the pine nuts are golden. Add the sherry vinegar and let bubble for 1 minute until nearly all the liquid has evaporated.
4 Return the drained spinach to the pan, season and toss together. Serve with the pork.

Serve with skin-on boiled new potatoes and a spoonful of smoked chilli jelly.

Jerk pork steaks with fruity salsa

Serves 2

2 tsp Caribbean/spicy seasoning
1 tbsp olive oil
4 pork loin steaks or chops, each
   about 150g
130g herb leaf salad, to serve

For the salsa

1 small, ripe mango, peeled, stoned
   and diced
1 ripe tomato, diced
1 dessert apple, cored and diced
2 tbsp freshly squeezed orange juice
1 tbsp mild olive oil
salt and pepper
small handful of fresh mint, chopped

1 Mix the Caribbean seasoning with the oil, then lightly smear the mixture all over the pork. Set aside.

2 Make the salsa. Put the diced mango into a bowl together with the tomato and apple. Add the orange juice and oil, season and mix together. Stir in the chopped mint.

3 Heat a large, non-stick frying pan. When hot, add the steaks and fry for 3–4 minutes on each side until golden and cooked through.

4 Remove from the heat, divide the steaks between two plates and serve with spoonfuls of salsa and a herb salad.

Pork & apple burgers with blue cheese

Serves 4

450g lean pork mince

1 red dessert apple, unpeeled, cored and finely diced

1 tsp paprika

salt and pepper

oil, for brushing

4 sesame burger buns, halved

130g mixed salad leaves

150g wedge blue cheese, sliced into 4 pieces

1 Tip the mince into a large bowl. Add the apple and paprika, season with salt and pepper and mix well with your hands. Shape into 4 round burgers, flattening them slightly.

2 Brush a griddle or frying pan with a little oil and place over a medium heat. When hot, add the burgers and cook for about 6 minutes then turn over and cook for a further 6 minutes or until browned and cooked through. Set aside to rest.

3 Brush the cut side of each bun with oil, then griddle each cut side for a few minutes until toasted.

4 Put some salad leaves on four bun bases. Top with a burger, then a slice of blue cheese. Sandwich together with the bun tops. Serve with coleslaw and oven chips.

To get ahead, shape the burgers the day before and keep covered in the fridge. Bring them back to room temperature before cooking.

Pork kebabs on minted broad beans with feta

Serves 4

1 pork tenderloin, about 450g,
   trimmed and cut into 12 pieces
12 cooked new potatoes
juice of ½ lemon
2 tbsp olive oil
small handful of fresh finely
   chopped rosemary

500g fresh (or frozen and thawed)
   broad beans
salt and pepper
handful of fresh mint leaves
3 tbsp extra virgin olive oil
150g Feta cheese, crumbled

1 Preheat the grill or barbecue. Thread three chunks of pork and three cooked baby new potatoes alternately onto each of four metal skewers.

2 Mix the lemon juice, olive oil and finely chopped rosemary together in a bowl and use to brush over the kebabs.

3 Cook the kebabs under the hot grill or on the barbecue for 10–12 minutes, turning once.

4 Meanwhile, boil the broad beans in a small saucepan of salted water for 4–5 minutes until just tender, then drain and refresh. Toss with a good handful of fresh mint leaves, the extra virgin olive oil, seasoning and the crumbled Feta. Divide between four plates and serve with the kebabs on top.

Pork chops with prunes & crème fraîche

Serves 4
4 pork chops or loin steaks, each
    about 150g
salt and pepper
knob of butter
200g ready-to-eat prunes, stoned and
    halved
100ml white wine
200ml carton crème fraîche

1 Season the pork chops with salt and pepper. Add a knob of butter to a large frying pan and place over a high heat. When hot, add the pork chops and cook for 2–3 minutes on each side to brown all over.
2 Add the prunes and white wine and boil to reduce by half. Stir in the crème fraîche and simmer for 2–3 minutes or until the pork is cooked through and the sauce thickened. Season and divide between four plates.

Delicious served with steamed curly kale and mashed potatoes.

Spiced lamb with apricots

Serves 2

250g lamb neck fillets, cut into
   chunks
1 small onion, chopped
1 tsp allspice
2 tbsp vegetable oil
salt and pepper

200g can chopped tomatoes
150ml hot chicken stock
75g ready-to-eat dried apricots
toasted flaked almonds, for
   sprinkling
lemon wedges, to serve (optional)

1 Put the lamb chunks into a bowl, add the chopped onion, the allspice and oil. Season and mix together.
2 Heat a large frying pan. When hot, add the lamb mixture and cook for 5 minutes to brown the meat and soften the onion. Stir in the chopped tomatoes, hot stock and apricots. Bring to the boil then simmer for 10 minutes until the lamb is cooked through and the sauce has thickened.
3 Season to taste, divide between two plates and sprinkle each with some toasted flaked almonds. Serve with steamed couscous and a lemon wedge, if you like.

Lamb chops with fennel & courgettes

Serves 4

2 tbsp olive oil

1 tsp butter

4 tbsp walnut pieces

2 fennel bulbs, thinly sliced into strips

3 medium green or yellow courgettes, sliced into chunky matchsticks

8 lamb chops, each about 75g

3 tbsp chopped fresh mint

zest of 1 lemon

1 tbsp lemon juice

salt and pepper

1 Preheat the grill to its highest setting. Heat the oil and butter in a large frying pan and, when sizzling, add the walnuts. Cook for 1 minute or until lightly toasted, then scoop into a bowl.

2 Add the fennel and courgettes to the pan and cook for 8–10 minutes over a medium heat until tender and slightly charred.

3 Meanwhile, put the lamb chops on a grill tray and cook under the grill for 8–10 minutes or until crispy, but still pink in the middle, turning halfway through.

4 Tip the cooked vegetables into a serving bowl and mix with the walnuts, mint, lemon zest and juice and seasoning. Serve with the lamb.

Serve with hot, buttered couscous or orzo (rice-shaped pasta).

Mustard & herb-crumbed lamb

Serves 4

2 tbsp finely chopped fresh rosemary

20g fresh flat-leaf parsley, leaves only, finely chopped

4 tbsp ready-made natural breadcrumbs

salt and pepper

2 heaped tbsp Dijon mustard

8 lamb chops (with a good fat layer)

20g butter

1 large leek, thinly sliced

240g frozen petits pois

150ml water

1 Preheat the oven to 220°C/fan oven 200°C/Gas 7. Combine the rosemary, parsley and breadcrumbs with a good grinding of salt and pepper and sprinkle onto a plate.

2 Using a knife, spread the Dijon mustard over the fat surrounding the lamb chops and over one side, then coat the mustardy sides with the herb mixture. Put onto a rack on a baking tray (breadcrumbed side uppermost) and roast for 20 minutes.

3 Meanwhile, melt the butter in a pan. Add the leek and sauté over a medium heat for 6–8 minutes or until tender. Add the peas, water and some seasoning, then bring to the boil, lower the heat and simmer for 3–4 minutes. Drain the leeks and peas and serve with the lamb chops.

Serve with some small boiled potatoes and redcurrant jelly.

Lamb patties with tzatziki

Illustrated on the following pages

Serves 4
220g couscous
500g fresh lamb mince
1 small courgette, grated
1 heaped tsp smoked paprika
salt

100g salad leaves
200g tzatziki
pinch each of chilli powder, ground
cumin, dried oregano and cayenne
pepper

1 Put the kettle on to boil for the couscous and heat a griddle pan until very hot.
2 Meanwhile, put the lamb mince into a large bowl and mix with the grated courgette, the smoked paprika and a generous seasoning of salt. Mix together and form into 12 small patties.
3 Griddle the patties for 3 minutes or until brown, then turn over and continue cooking for a further 3 minutes.
4 While the patties are cooking, prepare the couscous according to the packet instructions. When the couscous is cooked add the chilli powder, cumin, oregano and cayenne pepper and mix together until combined.
5 Serve the couscous topped with the lamb patties, some salad and a spoonful of tzatziki on the side.

Shaped into small patties, these spicy lamb burgers can also be served in warm flatbreads. If your griddle isn't non-stick, brush the burgers with a little oil before griddling.

Chicken breasts with tarragon & tagliatelle

Serves 4
4 skin-on chicken breasts
salt and pepper
small knob of butter
1 tbsp olive oil

1 ½ tbsp chopped fresh tarragon
squeeze of lemon juice
200ml crème fraîche
500g fresh garlic and herb
    tagliatelle or plain tagliatelle

1 Season the chicken with salt and pepper, then heat the butter and oil in a large frying pan. Brown the chicken breasts, skin-side down, for 5 minutes or until golden. Turn the chicken over and cook for a further 15–20 minutes over a medium heat.

2 Bring a large pan of salted water to the boil for the pasta. Meanwhile, stir the tarragon and lemon juice into the crème fraîche. Add the pasta to the boiling water and cook for 5 minutes.

3 Drain the excess fat from the frying pan, add the crème fraîche mixture to the pan and season. Simmer the chicken and sauce together for 2–3 minutes, then remove and slice the chicken.

4 Drain the pasta, return to the pan and toss with the sauce. Serve the pasta with the sliced chicken.

Chicken, ham & mustard pot pies

Serves 2

2 cooked chicken breasts, skinned and cut into small chunks

110g piece cooked smoked ham, cut into small chunks

1 tbsp grain mustard

1 tbsp chopped fresh parsley

2 tbsp frozen peas (no need to defrost)

375g ready-rolled fresh puff pastry

1 small egg yolk

For the sauce

275ml milk

25g plain flour

25g butter

50g mature Cheddar cheese, grated

salt and pepper

Note: You will need two 275ml pie dishes.

1 Preheat the oven to 200°C/fan oven 180°C/Gas 6. To make the sauce, put the milk, flour and butter into a medium pan and bring gently to a simmer, whisking constantly. Add the cheese, stir to melt and season.

2 Pour the sauce into a mixing bowl and mix with the chicken, ham, mustard, parsley and peas. Season with salt and pepper.

3 Using the rim of one of the 275ml pie dishes as a guide, cut out two rounds of pastry slightly bigger than the dishes. Divide the filling between each one, then brush the rims with a little of the egg yolk.

4 Cover each dish with a circle of pastry. Brush the tops with the remaining egg yolk. Place the dishes on a baking tray and bake for 15–20 minutes or until golden.

Keep the rest of the pastry for another time; it freezes well.

Chicken with lime, honey & chilli

Serves 2
3–4 chicken thighs, each about 125g
zest and juice of 2 limes
4 tbsp clear honey
1 fat garlic clove, crushed
½ tsp crushed dried chillies
salt

1 Preheat the oven to 240°C/fan oven 220°C/Gas 9. Put the chicken thighs in a single layer in a small roasting or baking dish.
2 Mix the lime zest and juice, honey, garlic and chillies together in a small bowl and season with salt. Pour the mixture over the chicken and turn the chicken thighs in the dish so they are coated.
3 Roast for 20–25 minutes, basting two or three times until the chicken thighs are sticky and golden all over.

Serve with white basmati rice and steamed pak choi.

Moroccan chicken with prunes & lemon

Serves 2

generous pinch each of ground
   cumin, coriander and chilli powder
2½ tbsp vegetable oil
salt and pepper
4 chicken thighs, with skin, each
   about 125g

8 ready-to-eat pitted prunes
1 small lemon, cut into 8 wedges
200g couscous
3 tbsp frozen petit pois
250ml hot vegetable stock
1 tsp butter
150ml natural yogurt, to serve

1 Mix the ground cumin, coriander and chilli powder with 2 tbsp of the oil and a pinch of salt and rub into the chicken thighs.
2 Heat the remaining oil in a large frying pan, add the chicken thighs, skin side down, and brown over a high heat. Turn the chicken over and scatter the prunes and lemon wedges on top. Cover and cook over a medium heat for 20 minutes, turning halfway through.
3 Shortly before serving, mix the couscous with the frozen peas in a bowl. Add the hot stock, stir, then cover and leave for 5 minutes. Stir in the butter, season and fluff with a fork.
4 Serve the chicken, prunes and lemon, leaving the excess oil in the pan, with the couscous and some yogurt.

Use ready-to-eat apricots rather than prunes, if you prefer.

Indonesian-style chicken couscous

Serves 4
four 150g skinless chicken breast
   fillets, cut into 8 large pieces
300g satay sauce
300g couscous
1 large red pepper, seeded and diced
350ml boiling water

3 tbsp crunchy peanut butter
1 bunch spring onions, finely sliced
salt and pepper

For the sauce
6 tbsp crunchy peanut butter
6 tbsp hot water

1 Put the chicken pieces in a non-metallic dish, add the satay sauce and mix until the chicken pieces are coated. Leave to marinate while soaking several wooden skewers in cold water for 30 minutes.

2 Put the couscous and diced red pepper into a large bowl. Pour the boiling water into a jug, stir in 3 tbsp crunchy peanut butter then stir into the couscous. Cover with cling film and set aside for 5 minutes until the liquid has been absorbed. Fluff up with a fork.

3 Add the marinated chicken pieces to the couscous together with the spring onions. Toss together, season to taste and divide between four plates.

4 To make the sauce, put the crunchy peanut butter in a small bowl and gradually stir in the hot water until it is quite runny. Drizzle over the couscous to serve.

Quick Thai green chicken curry

Serves 4
200ml carton coconut cream
3 tbsp Thai green curry paste
2 tbsp runny honey
juice of 1 lime
450g chicken breast fillets, sliced
handful of chopped fresh coriander

To garnish
chopped fresh coriander
1 red chilli, thinly sliced (optional)

1 Pour the coconut cream into a shallow non-metallic dish. Add the Thai green curry paste, honey and the lime juice and mix well. Add the chicken, toss together well and set aside for 15 minutes.

2 Transfer to a saucepan and gently simmer for 12–15 minutes until the chicken is cooked through and the sauce has thickened slightly. Add a handful of chopped coriander.

3 Garnish with more chopped coriander and thinly sliced red chilli, if you like, and serve with cooked basmati rice.

Honeyed duck & vegetable stir-fry

Illustrated on the previous pages

Serves 4

2 tbsp clear honey

4 tbsp dark soy sauce

4 skinless duck breasts, each about
200g, sliced

1 tbsp vegetable oil

2 carrots, peeled and cut into strips

1 bunch spring onions, cut into thin
strips

1 small head Chinese leaf, finely
shredded

salt and pepper

1 Mix the honey and soy sauce together in a large bowl. Add the duck to the honey marinade and toss until coated. Set aside for 5 minutes.

2 Heat the oil in a wok or large frying pan. Lift the duck from the marinade, reserving the marinade, and stir-fry for 2 minutes until browned all over. Remove and set aside.

3 Add the carrots to the wok or frying pan and stir-fry for 1 minute. Add the spring onions, Chinese leaf and browned duck. Pour over the marinade and stir-fry for 2–3 minutes. The duck should still be a little pink in the middle. Season to taste and serve with cooked Thai fragrant rice.

If you can't find any skinless duck breasts, buy duck breasts with skin and simply remove it yourself. This recipe works equally well with chicken breasts but make sure it is cooked through before serving.

Duck with fig, pine nut & mint couscous

Serves 3
2 large duck breasts
salt and pepper
225g couscous
handful of chopped ready-to-eat
 dried figs
275ml boiling water

40g pine nuts, toasted
handful of chopped fresh mint

To finish
chopped fresh mint
150g natural yogurt

1 Put a frying pan over a high heat. Score the skin of the duck breasts with a sharp knife and season all over. Add to the hot pan, skin-side down. Lower the heat to medium-low and cook for about 15 minutes, turning halfway and discarding the fat in the pan, until golden but still a little pink in the middle. Set the duck aside for 5 minutes, then slice diagonally.
2 Meanwhile, put the couscous in a bowl with the figs and season well. Pour over the boiling water, cover with clingfilm and set aside for 5 minutes.
3 Fluff the couscous grains with a fork and stir through the pine nuts and the chopped mint. Divide the couscous between three plates and top with the duck slices.
4 Stir a little chopped mint into the yogurt and serve with the duck.

fast
fish &
shellfish

Chilli squid salad with peanuts

Serves 2

2.5cm piece fresh root ginger, peeled
and finely chopped
2 tbsp sweet chilli sauce
juice of 1 lime
3–4 tbsp vegetable oil
6 small squid, halved lengthways
2 tbsp cornflour

salt and pepper
120g fresh herb salad
$\frac{1}{2}$ cucumber, halved, seeded and
thinly sliced
2 tbsp roasted salted peanuts,
chopped
300g bean sprouts

1 First, make a dressing by whisking together the ginger, chilli sauce, lime juice and 1 tbsp oil.
2 Score the squid in a criss-cross pattern and dry on kitchen paper, with the tentacles. Sprinkle the cornflour onto a plate and season.
3 Heat 2 tbsp oil in a large frying pan until sizzling. Toss the squid in the cornflour and add to the pan. Stir-fry for 2–3 minutes, adding more oil if necessary.
4 Put the salad into a large bowl and mix with the cucumber, peanuts and bean sprouts. Add the hot squid and toss with the dressing. Serve immediately.

Serve this quick stir-fry on its own or with steamed rice.

Sweet-&-sour prawns with lime

Makes 4

16 large raw prawns, shelled and
  deveined
2 tbsp olive oil
1 garlic clove, crushed
2 tbsp light soy sauce

1–2 tbsp clear honey
2 limes
2 tbsp roughly chopped fresh
  coriander
pinch of chilli flakes
salt and pepper

Note: You will need four wooden or bamboo skewers.

1 Soak the skewers in cold water for at least 30 minutes. Light the barbecue according to the manufacturer's instructions.
2 Meanwhile, rinse the prawns and pat dry on kitchen paper. Put into a bowl and set aside. Mix the oil, garlic, soy sauce, honey, the zest and juice of 1 lime, coriander, chilli flakes and seasoning. Pour over the prawns and toss well. Cover and marinate in the fridge for 15 minutes.
3 Cut the remaining lime into quarters. Thread 4 prawns and a lime wedge onto each presoaked skewer. Barbecue directly over a medium heat source for 2–3 minutes, turning halfway and brushing with any remaining marinade, until pink and tender. Serve with a tomato salad.

You could cook these under a medium-hot grill for 8–10 minutes, turning once.

Prawns with mango & avocado

Serves 4 for a light lunch or starter

8 tbsp mild olive oil
juice of ½ orange
handful of chopped fresh coriander
   leaves, plus extra leaves to garnish
salt and pepper
1 ripe mango
2 ripe avocados
300g cooked and shelled large
   prawns, with tail-shells on

1 Mix the oil, orange juice and chopped coriander together in a small bowl to make a dressing. Season and set aside.
2 Peel, stone and slice the mango and set aside. Halve, stone and peel the avocados, discarding the skin. Slice the flesh and divide between four plates, along with the mango and prawns. Season to taste.
3 Drizzle each plate with the coriander dressing then scatter with a few coriander leaves to serve.

Clams with pea shoots & wild garlic

Serves 4

2kg fresh clams, in their shells
1 tbsp vegetable oil
1 bunch spring onions, sliced
leaves from 4–5 fresh thyme sprigs
200g fresh or frozen garden peas,
   thawed if frozen
1 tbsp shaoxing rice wine or dry
   sherry
1 tbsp rice vinegar or white wine
   vinegar

250ml fresh hot vegetable stock
about 100g snow pea shoots or
   watercress, washed and
   thoroughly drained
about 100g wild garlic leaves or 25g
   garlic chives, roughly chopped
dash of soy sauce (optional)
pinch of salt (optional)

1 Wash the clams under cold running water, then discard any with broken or open shells. Set aside.
2 Heat the oil in a wok or large saucepan. As soon as it is hot, add the spring onions, thyme and garden peas. Stir-fry for 1 minute, then add the clams, wine or sherry, vinegar and stock. Cover and steam for 3–4 minutes or until all the shells open. Discard any that stay shut.
3 Uncover, add the pea shoots or watercress and garlic leaves or chives and cook until just wilted. Check the seasoning – you could add a dash of soy or pinch of salt – and serve.

Garlic chives or kow choi are available from Asian supermarkets. If you cannot buy these use ordinary fresh chives instead.

Mussels with wine
& basil tomatoes

Illustrated on the following pages

Serves 2

1 tbsp olive oil

1 onion, finely chopped

150ml dry white wine

400g can chopped tomatoes

pepper

900g fresh mussels, cleaned

handful of fresh basil leaves, torn,
   plus extra to garnish

1 Heat the oil in a deep saucepan over a medium heat. Add the onion and
cook, stirring, for 3–4 minutes. Pour in the wine and cook to reduce by half.
2 Stir in the chopped tomatoes, season with pepper and simmer rapidly for
5 minutes. Add the mussels to the tomato sauce together with the basil
leaves. Cover and cook for 4–5 minutes, shaking the pan occasionally, until
the mussels have opened. Discard any that remain shut.
3 Divide the mussels between two large bowls and garnish with more fresh
basil. Serve with crusty bread or thinly cut chips and plenty of napkins.

Fish & chips
with herby dip

Serves 2

250g lemon sole fillets, skinned

1 small egg

salt and pepper

50g ready-made natural
  breadcrumbs

350g ready-made oven chips

6 tbsp mayonnaise

1 tbsp snipped fresh chives

1 tbsp lemon juice

1 Preheat the oven to 220°C/fan oven 200°C/Gas 7. Slice the sole fillets into
7.5 x 2.5cm strips.

2 Beat the egg with a little salt and pepper in a medium-size bowl, and
scatter the breadcrumbs over a large plate.

3 Put the chips onto a large baking tray and bake for 10 minutes. While the
chips are cooking, dip the sole pieces first in the egg and then in the crumbs
so each strip is coated. Remove the baking tray from the oven, turn the
chips and add the coated fish strips. Bake for a further 10 minutes until
crisp and brown.

4 Mix the mayonnaise, chives, lemon juice and seasoning together in a small
bowl. Serve the fish and chips, sprinkled with a little salt, with the sauce
for dipping.

Smoked mackerel & chorizo potatoes

Serves 4

200g piece chorizo sausage, roughly chopped
2 small onions, chopped
900g potatoes, cut into small cubes
250g cherry tomatoes, halved
4 peppered smoked mackerel fillets, skinned
large handful of fresh parsley leaves, chopped

1 Heat a large, non-stick frying pan over a high heat. Add the chorizo and cook, stirring, for 2 minutes until most of the oil has been released. Remove with a slotted spoon and set aside.
2 Lower the heat to medium and add the onions and potatoes to the pan. Coat in the oil from the chorizo and cook for 12 minutes, stirring occasionally or until the potatoes are just tender and the onions golden.
3 Stir the tomatoes and chorizo into the pan. Flake the mackerel fillets with a fork and add them to the pan. Gently mix and cook for 2 minutes until piping hot. Stir in the parsley. Divide between four plates and serve with a mixed leaf salad.

This dish will freeze for up to a month. Thaw overnight, then pan-fry in a little oil over a high heat until everything's piping hot.

Chargrilled mackerel with balsamic tomatoes

Illustrated on the following pages

Serves 2

2 tbsp olive oil
2 shallots, finely chopped
1 fat garlic clove, sliced
250g pomodorino tomatoes,
 quartered

4 mackerel fillets, each about 100g
salt and pepper
200g tenderstem broccoli, trimmed
2 tbsp vintage balsamic vinegar

1 Preheat a griddle pan. Heat half the oil in a frying pan and fry the shallots and garlic over a low heat for 4–5 minutes or until softened.
2 Add the tomatoes to the frying pan with the shallots and garlic and simmer for 2–3 minutes.
3 Meanwhile, brush the mackerel fillets on both sides with oil and season with pepper. Griddle for 4–5 minutes, turning halfway through.
4 Cook the broccoli in a pan of boiling salted water for 3–4 minutes or until tender, then drain. Remove the tomato mixture from the heat, stir in the balsamic vinegar and season. Serve with the mackerel and broccoli.

This dish incorporates tomatoes, which offer a great source of lycopene and beta-carotene, mackerel, rich in omega-3 fatty acids, and broccoli, containing folic acid – all of which help beat stress and release tension.

Mackerel, tomato & mustard tart

Serves 4
375g ready-rolled puff pastry
plain flour, for dusting
240g peppered smoked mackerel
  fillets

1 tbsp wholegrain mustard
6 tbsp crème fraîche
4 large ripe tomatoes, cut into
  8 wedges
3 tbsp chopped fresh parsley

1 Preheat the oven to 220°C/fan oven 200°C/Gas 7. Unroll the pastry on to a large lightly floured board and score a line on it all the way round, 2.5cm in from the edge. Prick all over the centre of the pastry with a fork and bake for 10 minutes.
2 Meanwhile, break the mackerel into small chunks, discarding the skin as you do so. Mix the mustard and crème fraîche together in a small bowl.
3 Remove the pastry from the oven and push down the centre with the back of a fork. Spread the crème fraîche mixture over the centre of the pastry and then scatter the mackerel, tomatoes and parsley on top. Return the tart to the oven for 12–15 minutes or until bubbling.

Remember to take the puff pastry out of the fridge 20 minutes before using.

Hot crab ramekins

Serves 4

25g butter
110g mushrooms, finely chopped
1 level tbsp plain flour
2 tbsp white wine
200ml milk
75g Cheddar cheese, grated
1 tsp Dijon mustard

salt and pepper
2 tbsp double cream
295g brown and white crabmeat,
   or 2 dressed crabs
50g Parmesan cheese, grated
1 rounded tbsp fresh breadcrumbs
lemon wedges, to serve (optional)

1 Melt the butter in a small saucepan. Add the mushrooms and sauté for 3–4 minutes over a low heat. Add the flour and stir over the heat for about 1 minute. Add the wine and cook for a further 2 minutes. Stir in the milk and cook for 3–4 minutes.

2 Add 50g of the Cheddar cheese, the mustard and some seasoning. Stir to melt, then add the cream and the crabmeat and cook for 1–2 minutes.

3 Spoon the mixture into four ramekins. Mix the remaining Cheddar, the Parmesan and breadcrumbs together and sprinkle over the crab. If not serving straight away, chill in the fridge until needed.

4 When ready to serve, warm through in a hot oven for about 5 minutes, then grill under a preheated hot grill until brown and bubbling. Serve with a lemon wedge and brown bread, if you like.

Kedgeree

Illustrated on the following pages

Serves 2

1 tbsp olive oil

1 tsp each cumin and fennel seeds,
  lightly crushed

1 small onion, finely chopped

200g basmati rice

400ml cold water

150g frozen garden peas

300g undyed smoked haddock
  fillets, skinned

15g butter

2 medium eggs

5 tbsp single cream

salt and pepper

small handful of chopped fresh flat-
  leaf parsley (optional)

1 Heat the oil in a medium non-stick saucepan over a low heat. Add the spices and onion and sauté for 5 minutes until softened.

2 Rinse the rice under cold running water until the water runs clear, then tip into the saucepan and stir until coated in the oil. Pour over the cold water and scatter with the frozen peas. Arrange the whole haddock fillets on top and place the butter over the fish. Bring to the boil, then cover with a tight-fitting lid and cook over the lowest possible heat for 12 minutes.

3 Meanwhile, place two eggs in a small pan of cold water. Bring to the boil and boil for 6 minutes. Remove and set aside to cool slightly. Remove the shells and cut the eggs into quarters.

4 Remove the lid from the kedgeree pan and increase the heat to drive off any excess moisture.

5 Lower the heat and flake the fish with a fork, stir in the single cream and warm through. Season well, top with the egg quarters and parsley, if using, and serve.

Smoked haddock with Florentine sauce

Serves 2

225g young-leaf spinach
pinch of freshly grated nutmeg
salt and pepper
250g skinless smoked haddock
300g ready-made cheese sauce
   (see page 91)
3 tbsp freshly grated Parmesan
   cheese

1 Preheat the grill to its highest setting. Microwave the spinach leaves according to the packet instructions. Alternatively, wilt them in a pan for 2–3 minutes. Squeeze out any excess water from the spinach leaves and spread them over the base of a 23 x 19 x 4cm ovenproof dish. Season with nutmeg, salt and pepper.
2 Place the smoked haddock fillets on top, followed by the cheese sauce and the Parmesan cheese.
3 Grill for 12–15 minutes or until hot and golden.

Roast spiced cod with mango & lime

Serves 4

1½ tsp garam masala
1 tsp turmeric
salt
1 lime
275g white basmati rice
1 tbsp olive oil, plus extra for rice

550ml water
4 cod loins, about 630g total
1 medium red chilli, seeded and
    finely chopped
1 medium mango
20g fresh coriander, leaves only,
    chopped

1 Preheat the oven to 200°C/fan oven 180°C/Gas 6. Mix the spices and a generous pinch of salt together. Slice the lime into six pieces, discarding the ends, then cut each slice in half.

2 To cook the rice, heat a little oil in a pan, stir in the rice and add the water. Cook for about 15 minutes or until tender. Alternatively, cook the rice according to the packet instructions.

3 Arrange the four cod loins in a small roasting tin and drizzle with the oil. Sprinkle some spice mixture onto each piece of fish and arrange the lime slices on top. Sprinkle with the chilli and roast for 8–10 minutes.

4 Keeping the skin on, cut off the flesh of the mango on either side of the stone. Cut each 'cheek' into four wedges. When the cod has been in the oven for 4 minutes, add the wedges to the tin and roast for the remaining cooking time.

5 Drain the rice, mix with the chopped coriander and serve with the fish.

There's lots of flavour in this spicy dish, plus it's a low fat option.

Salmon fishfingers

Makes 12
juice and grated zest of ½ lemon,
   plus wedges to serve
2 salmon fillets, about 350g, skinned
600g cold cooked mashed potato
1 tbsp chopped fresh herbs, such as
   chives or parsley (optional)

5 tbsp sesame seeds
5 tbsp linseeds
3 tbsp olive oil
lemon wedges, to serve

1 Drizzle the lemon juice over the salmon fillets. Microwave on high (900W) for 3 minutes until the fish is tender and flakes easily after standing for a few minutes. Drain off any liquid.

2 Flake the fish into a bowl, then add the cold mashed potato, herbs, if using, and lemon zest and mix together well.

3 Line a baking sheet with baking paper and sprinkle with 3 tbsp each of the sesame seeds and linseeds. Top with the salmon mixture and use a palette knife to flatten to 2.5cm deep, with neat square edges. Cut into 12 chunky fishfingers, separating them out a little. Sprinkle over the remaining seeds. Cover and pop in the freezer for 15 minutes to firm up, or freeze completely for another day.

4 Preheat the oven to 220°C/fan oven 200°C/Gas 7. Drizzle the fishfingers with oil and cook for 15 minutes or 20–25 minutes from frozen. Serve with a lemon wedge, broccoli, peas and thinly cut chips.

These fishfingers can be prepared in advance and cooked from frozen, so it's worth making lots in one go.

Thai-poached salmon

Serves 2

125g long-grain rice
salt
1 tbsp Thai red or green curry paste
200ml carton coconut cream
2 skinless salmon fillets, each
    about 150g
100g fine green beans, trimmed
handful of fresh coriander leaves,
    plus extra to garnish

1 Cook the rice in a pan of boiling salted water for about 12–15 minutes
until tender, then drain. Alternatively cook the rice according to the
packet instructions.
2 Meanwhile, heat a medium frying pan. Add the curry paste and cook,
stirring, for a few seconds. Gradually stir in the coconut cream and bring to
a simmer. Add the salmon fillets, cover and simmer for 7–8 minutes, turning
the fish over halfway.
3 Meanwhile, blanch the green beans in a pan of simmering water until just
tender. Drain and divide between two hot serving plates. Stir the coriander
into the sauce. Top the beans with the salmon, spooning over the sauce.
Garnish with extra coriander and serve with the cooked rice.

Plaice with mushrooms & Parmesan

Serves 2

small knob of butter, plus extra for
  greasing
250g closed-cup chestnut
  mushrooms, sliced
salt and pepper

4 large skinless plaice fillets, about
  315g once skinned
2 tsp olive oil
squeeze of lemon juice
2 tbsp freshly grated Parmesan
  cheese

1 Preheat the grill to its highest setting. Melt the knob of butter in a frying pan and when sizzling, add the mushrooms and cook for 7–8 minutes or until tender. Season well.

2 Meanwhile, arrange the plaice fillets in a lightly greased medium-size ovenproof dish in a single layer. Drizzle with the oil and lemon juice, season and grill for 4 minutes.

3 Scatter the mushrooms over the fish and sprinkle with the Parmesan cheese. Return to the grill for a further 3–4 minutes until the Parmesan has turned golden and is bubbling. Serve immediately with some boiled, buttered new potatoes and steamed tenderstem broccoli.

This will also work well with cod – just increase the cooking time slightly to accommodate the thicker fillet.

Steamed hoki with lime, chilli & ginger

Serves 2
400g hoki fillets
2 tbsp light soy sauce
2 tbsp vegetable stock
1 tsp sesame oil
1 tsp caster sugar

1 lime, thinly sliced
1 red chilli, seeded and sliced
5cm piece fresh root ginger, peeled
   and sliced
3 spring onions, sliced

1 Preheat the oven to 200°C/fan oven 180°C/Gas 6. Place the hoki fillets on 2 double-thickness squares of foil, measuring about 28cm square.
2 Mix the soy, stock, oil and sugar together and sprinkle half over each. Top the fillets with the lime slices and sprinkle over the chilli, ginger and spring onion. Close up the parcels loosely and place on a baking tray.
3 Bake for 15 minutes, then leave to rest, unopened, for 5 minutes. Serve with jasmine rice and steamed pak choi.

This recipe will work with any other firm, white fish fillets.

Grilled flat fish with herb & caper dressing

Serves 4

4 x 450–500g lemon sole, plaice,
    flounder, megrim or witch sole
olive oil, for brushing
sea salt flakes

For the dressing

1 garlic clove, finely chopped
15g fresh flat leaf parsley leaves,
    chopped
10g fresh mint leaves, chopped
3 tbsp capers, drained, rinsed and
    chopped
15g anchovy fillets (about 4) in olive
    oil, drained and finely chopped
1 tsp Dijon mustard
1½ tbsp fresh lemon juice
120ml extra virgin olive oil

1 Preheat the grill to high. To make the dressing, mix all the ingredients in a bowl and season to taste with salt. Set aside.

2 To close-cut a flat fish, put the fish onto a board and run your fingers down either side of the fish, close to the frills. You will feel a very slight indentation in the flesh, which runs between the frills and adjacent fillet of fish. Cut along this indentation either side of the fish with kitchen scissors, cutting away the frills and about 1cm of the adjacent flesh. You will be left with quite a long, thin fish. Make a series of deep cuts into the flesh on the darker side of the fish.

3 Brush both sides of the fish with oil and season both sides with sea salt flakes. Place dark-side up on the rack of the grill pan. If your grill pan isn't large enough, cook 2 at a time and keep warm in a low oven.

4 Grill the fish for 8–10 minutes on one side only until cooked through. To check if it is ready, make a small cut in the thickest part of the fillet, just behind the head: it should be firm and opaque close to the bone and show signs of the flesh coming away from the bones quite easily. If it is still a bit pink, grill for a further 2 minutes.

5 Lift the cooked fish onto warmed plates, spoon over some dressing and serve with thinly cut chips.

Pan-fried fish fillets with crispy bacon

Serves 4

8 thin-cut rindless streaky bacon
  rashers
25g plain flour
salt and pepper
2 tbsp sunflower oil
45g unsalted butter

8 x 75g or 12 x 50g skinned Dover
  sole, lemon sole, plaice, flounder,
  megrim or witch sole fillets
2 tsp fresh lemon juice
1 tsp each finely chopped fresh
  tarragon, parsley and chives

1 Preheat the grill to high. Lay the bacon rashers on the grill rack and set aside.

2 Put the flour onto a shallow tray and season. Put half the oil and 10g butter into a large frying pan and melt the butter over a low heat.

3 Meanwhile, dip the fillets into the seasoned flour, making sure they are well coated on both sides. Shake off the excess.

4 Grill the bacon until crisp and golden, then keep warm.

5 Meanwhile, increase the heat under the frying pan. When the butter starts foaming add half the fillets and fry over a medium-high heat for 2 minutes on each side until lightly golden. Put the cooked fillets on a plate and keep warm. Wipe out the pan and cook the other fillets, using the rest of the oil and another 10g butter.

6 Wipe out the pan with kitchen paper and return to a medium heat with the remaining butter. When the butter has melted and starts to go pale brown, add the lemon juice and herbs and remove from the heat. Season. Arrange the fillets and bacon on warmed plates, spoon over some beurre noisette and serve.

fast
pasta,
gnocchi,
rice &
noodles

Boccoletti with prawns, peas & beans

Serves 4

375g dried boccoletti or penne
salt and pepper
200g frozen petit pois
110g extra-fine beans, halved
220g cooked shelled large king
  prawns

25g fresh flat leaf parsley, leaves
  only
15g fresh basil, leaves only
zest of 1 small lemon
juice of ½ lemon
200ml carton crème fraîche

1 Cook the pasta in a large pan of boiling salted water until al dente. Four minutes or so before the end of its cooking time, add the frozen peas and beans to the pan.

2 Drain the pasta and vegetables then return to the pan over a low heat. Add the prawns, parsley, basil, lemon zest and juice and crème fraîche and seasoning. Heat through for 4–5 minutes or until piping hot.

Conchiglie with haddock & broccoli

Serves 4
2 tbsp olive oil
4 smoked streaky bacon rashers, chopped
2 garlic cloves, finely chopped
350g dried conchiglie
salt and pepper

250g broccoli florets, cut into smaller florets
200ml carton crème fraîche
400g smoked haddock, skinned and cut into large pieces
zest and juice of 1 small lemon

1 Heat the olive oil in a frying pan over a high heat. Add the bacon and cook for 2 minutes, then add the garlic and cook until the bacon is crisp.

2 Cook the pasta in a large pan of boiling salted water for 10–12 minutes or until al dente. Towards the end of the cooking time, add the broccoli to the pasta water and cook for 3–4 minutes.

3 Meanwhile, add the crème fraîche to the frying pan and heat until melted. Stir in the smoked haddock and cook over a medium heat for 2–3 minutes or until opaque and cooked through.

4 Drain the pasta and broccoli and return to the pan with the haddock mixture, together with the lemon zest and juice. Toss together and season.

Penne with pancetta, mozzarella & basil

Serves 2

200g dried penne

salt

160g cubed pancetta

2 fat garlic cloves, finely chopped

240g carton sunblush tomatoes,
  drained

generous pinch of dried crushed
  chilli flakes

150g mozzarella cheese, cubed

20g fresh basil leaves, roughly torn
  into small pieces

50g wild rocket leaves

1 Cook the pasta in a large pan of boiling salted water for 10–12 minutes or until al dente.

2 Meanwhile, heat a frying pan and, when hot, add the pancetta and fry for 3–4 minutes or until golden. Add the garlic and cook for a further minute, stirring. Stir in the drained sunblush tomatoes, together with the chilli flakes. Stir and remove the pan from the heat.

3 Drain the pasta, then return it to the pan. Add the pancetta mixture, the mozzarella, basil and rocket and toss together over the heat until the cheese starts to melt. Serve immediately.

Penne with artichokes, goats' cheese & olives

Serves 2
175g dried penne
salt and pepper
400g can artichoke hearts in brine,
   drained and thinly sliced
20 pitted Kalamata olives

100g goats' cheese, cut into
   small cubes
juice of ½ small lemon
3 tbsp olive oil
20g fresh flat leaf parsley, chopped

1 Cook the pasta in a large pan of boiling salted water for 10–12 minutes or until al dente.
2 Mix the sliced artichoke hearts, olives, cheese, lemon juice, oil and parsley in a bowl.
3 Drain the pasta, keeping 1 tbsp of the cooking water in the pan. Return the pasta to the pan, then mix with the rest of the ingredients and season. Return to the heat for 2 minutes until the cheese just starts to melt. Serve in two warmed bowls.

Penne with sausage, fennel & garlic

Serves 4
400g good quality pork sausages
2 tbsp olive oil
1 onion, finely sliced
2 fat garlic cloves, finely chopped

1 tsp fennel seeds
400g dried penne
salt and pepper
200ml carton crème fraîche
100g wild rocket leaves

1 Heat a frying pan. Cut each sausage into five chunks and cook them over a high heat for 8–10 minutes until golden and cooked through.

2 Meanwhile, heat the oil in a frying pan. Fry the sliced onions for 5 minutes. Add the garlic and fennel seeds and cook for a further 5 minutes.

3 Cook the pasta in a large pan of boiling salted water for 8–10 minutes or until al dente. Drain the pasta and return to the pan with the sausages, onion mixture, crème fraîche, rocket and some salt and pepper and heat gently for 2 minutes before serving.

You can use any short pasta for this recipe.

Orechiette with chicken & artichokes

Illustrated on the previous pages

Serves 4

375g dried orechiette
salt and pepper
1 tbsp olive oil
1 onion, chopped
4 skinless chicken breast fillets, each
   about 150g, cut into 1cm strips

200g cherry tomatoes, halved
290g jar chargrilled artichoke
   hearts in oil, drained and halved
95g ready-made wild rocket or
   basil pesto
85g wild rocket leaves

1 Cook the pasta in a large pan of boiling salted water for 8–10 minutes or until al dente.

2 Meanwhile, heat the oil in a large frying pan, add the onion and fry over a medium heat for 3 minutes. Increase the heat, add the chicken and continue to cook for a further 8–10 minutes until golden on both sides.

3 Add the tomatoes and stir-fry for 1 minute before adding the artichokes and pesto. Warm through, then toss with the drained pasta, the rocket and some seasoning.

Pasta bake with sausage & spinach

Illustrated on the following pages

Serves 4
1 tbsp olive oil
400g Sicilian or pork sausages
315g dried fusilli
salt

1 red pepper, seeded and chopped
500g ready-made cheese sauce
225g young-leaf spinach
150g mozzarella cheese, roughly
  torn

1 Heat the oil in a frying pan. Remove the sausages' skins and add the meat to the pan, breaking it up with a wooden spoon.
2 Meanwhile, cook the pasta in a large pan of boiling salted water for about 8–10 minutes or until al dente.
3 Add the chopped pepper to the frying pan and fry with the sausages for about 12–15 minutes until the pepper is soft and the meat has browned.
4 Preheat the grill to high. Heat the cheese sauce in a small pan or in the microwave until hot.
5 Drain the pasta, retaining 2 tbsp of the cooking water. Return the drained pasta to the pan with the hot cheese sauce and half of the spinach. Warm gently, stirring until the spinach has wilted, then add the remaining spinach and the reserved pasta cooking water and stir together.
6 Spoon half of the pasta into the base of an ovenproof dish. Scatter over half of the sausage and pepper mixture and then add the remaining pasta. Top with the rest of the sausage mixture. Scatter the torn mozzarella over the top and grill until the cheese has melted and is beginning to brown.

Linguine with a fresh tomato & olive sauce

Serves 4

5 vine-ripened tomatoes, seeded and finely diced
2 tbsp extra virgin olive oil
50g wild rocket leaves, roughly chopped
100g marinated green and black pitted olives, roughly chopped
salt and pepper
400g dried linguine or spaghetti
75g grated Gruyère cheese, plus extra to serve

1 Put the tomatoes into a bowl, add the olive oil, rocket and roughly chopped olives. Season and set aside.

2 Cook the pasta in a large pan of boiling salted water for 8–10 minutes or until al dente. Drain and add to the tomato mix together with the grated Gruyère cheese, tossing to coat.

3 Serve the pasta in warmed bowls with a grinding of black pepper and a little extra grated cheese on top.

Linguine with asparagus & pancetta

Serves 2

160g cubed pancetta

2 garlic cloves, crushed

generous pinch of dried chilli flakes

100g asparagus tips, halved
  lengthways

salt and pepper

225g dried linguine or spaghetti

grated zest of 1 lemon

2 tbsp lemon juice

2 tbsp extra virgin olive oil

2–3 tbsp each chopped fresh basil
  and mint leaves

1 Heat a frying pan and when hot, cook the pancetta in its own fat until crisp and brown. Add the garlic and chilli flakes and cook for about 30 seconds, then set aside.

2 Cook the asparagus in a pan of boiling salted water for 1–2 minutes or until just tender. Using a slotted spoon, transfer the asparagus to a sieve and place under cold running water until cool. At the same time, add the pasta to the pan of boiling water and cook for 8–10 minutes or until al dente.

3 Drain the pasta and return it to the pan with the pancetta mixture, lemon zest and juice, olive oil, basil and mint leaves, and the asparagus, and season lightly with salt. Toss together over a gentle heat and serve with a grinding of black pepper.

Linguine with leeks, bacon, ciabatta & chilli

Serves 4
4 tbsp olive oil
½ ciabatta loaf, cut into small cubes
generous pinch of crushed dried
  chillies
1 garlic clove, finely chopped
sea salt

400g dried linguine or spaghetti
225g dry-cure smoked streaky bacon
  rashers, chopped
450g or 4 medium trimmed leeks,
  sliced

1 Heat half of the oil in a large frying pan. Add the ciabatta cubes and toss
the cubes in the hot oil for 4–5 minutes or until golden, adding the chilli,
garlic and a sprinkling of sea salt towards the end. Tip into a bowl.
2 Meanwhile, cook the pasta in a large pan of boiling salted water for about
8–10 minutes or until al dente. Add the rest of the oil to the frying pan and
cook the chopped bacon until crispy. Stir in the leeks and cook for a further
8–10 minutes or until softened.
3 Drain the pasta, reserving 2 tbsp of the cooking water, then return to the
pan with the cooking water liquid, the bacon and leek mixture and the
ciabatta croûtons. Toss together and serve.

Crab linguine with chilli, lemon & garlic

Illustrated on the following pages

Serves 4

100ml olive oil

1 medium-hot red chilli, seeded and finely chopped

1 fat garlic clove, finely chopped

3 pared strips of lemon zest, finely chopped

salt and pepper

450g dried linguine

2 tbsp lemon juice

225g freshly cooked white crabmeat

2 tbsp chopped fresh flat leaf parsley

lemon wedges, to serve

1 Put the olive oil, chilli, garlic and lemon zest into a small pan and set over a gentle heat until it begins to sizzle. Remove from the heat and set aside.

2 Bring a large saucepan of well salted water to the boil. Add the linguine and cook for 8–10 minutes or until al dente. Drain well and set aside.

3 Tip the chilli and lemon mixture into the pan the pasta was in, then add the lemon juice and season. Heat until sizzling, then add the linguine and crabmeat to the pan and toss gently over a medium heat to warm the crabmeat through.

4 Add the parsley, season and serve immediately with lemon wedges.

Ravioli with butternut, sage & pine nuts

Serves 2–3

350g butternut squash, peeled and
  cut into small chunks

75g pine nuts

300g ready-made fresh pumpkin
  ravioli or other fresh stuffed pasta

salt and pepper

12 fresh sage leaves

50g butter

1 Cook the butternut chunks in a steamer for 6–8 minutes or until just tender.

2 Toast the pine nuts in a small frying pan for 2–3 minutes or until golden. Set aside.

3 Cook the ravioli in a large pan of boiling salted water for 5 minutes.

4 Chop most of the sage leaves, reserving a few for the garnish. Add the butter to the frying pan and heat until it turns a nut brown colour, adding the sage at the end so it frizzles slightly.

5 Drain the pasta and then return it to the pan. Add the butternut chunks, sage butter, pine nuts and some salt and pepper to the pan and toss together over a low heat. Serve garnished with a few sage leaves.

Tortellini with lemon & courgette

Serves 2

25g pine nuts

250g goats' cheese and pesto
   tortellini or other cheese-stuffed
   pasta shapes

50g butter

1 large courgette, roughly grated

1 garlic clove, crushed

juice of ½ lemon

salt and pepper

fresh basil leaves, for sprinkling

1 Cook the pine nuts in a hot, dry non-stick frying pan until golden. Remove from the pan and set aside.

2 Cook the tortellini in a large pan of boiling water for about 3 minutes or until cooked through. Drain and set aside.

3 Melt the butter in the frying pan, add the grated courgette and crushed garlic and cook for 1–2 minutes, stirring. Stir in the lemon juice and cook for 30 seconds.

4 Remove from the heat, add the cooked tortellini and toss well. Season to taste. Divide between two plates and scatter with the toasted pine nuts and basil leaves to serve.

Green bean, tomato, spinach & Feta pasta

Serves 2

25g pine nuts
100g fine green beans, trimmed
250g dried pasta, such as conchiglie
   (shells)
salt and pepper
100g baby spinach leaves

150g cherry tomatoes, halved
3 tbsp ready-made balsamic vinegar
   and olive oil dressing
100g Feta cheese
small handful of fresh basil leaves,
   to garnish

1 Dry-fry the pine nuts in a large saucepan for 1–2 minutes until golden, then remove and set aside.

2 Using the same pan, fill with cold water and bring to the boil. Add the beans and blanch for 2 minutes. Remove with a slotted spoon and refresh under cold running water. This will help them keep their bright green colour. Set aside.

3 Add the pasta and a pinch of salt to the boiling water and cook for 8–10 minutes or until al dente. Drain and briefly run under cold running water to cool slightly, then return to the pan.

4 Put the spinach leaves in a colander and pour over a kettle of boiling water to wilt them. Refresh under cold running water, then squeeze out as much excess water as you can. Toss the spinach through the pasta, then add the beans, tomatoes and dressing. Season.

5 Divide between two bowls. Sprinkle with the toasted pine nuts and crumble over the Feta. Scatter with basil leaves to garnish and serve.

Olive, chorizo & tomato pasta

Serves 2 generously

250g fresh pasta, such as trompetti
400g can cherry tomatoes
125g ball mozzarella cheese, drained
  and chopped
100g chorizo, chopped

75g pitted large green olives
salt and pepper
150ml boiling water
freshly grated Parmesan cheese,
  to serve

1 Preheat the oven to 200°C/fan oven 180°C/Gas 6. Tip the fresh pasta into two individual dishes or a medium-size baking dish, then pour over the cherry tomatoes. Add the chopped mozzarella, chorizo and olives. Season, pour in the boiling water and mix together.
2 Cover tightly with foil, then bake in the oven for 20 minutes until piping hot and the pasta is cooked through.
3 Divide between two plates and serve with freshly grated Parmesan cheese.

Gnocchi with peppers, spinach & mozzarella

Serves 4
1 tbsp olive oil
1 red and 1 yellow pepper, seeded
   and cut into large chunks
500g fresh gnocchi
225g young-leaf spinach
350g ready-made fresh
   Mediterranean vegetable and
   rosemary pasta sauce or other
   vegetable pasta sauce

20g fresh basil, leaves only, roughly
   chopped
salt and pepper
150ml water
150g mozzarella cheese, thinly sliced
2 tbsp freshly grated Parmesan
   cheese

1 Heat the oil in a large pan. Add the peppers and cook for 6–8 minutes, covering with a lid but stirring occasionally until soft.
2 Preheat the grill to high. Cook the gnocchi for 3 minutes in a pan of boiling water, then drain.
3 Stir the spinach into the peppers in two batches, leaving it to wilt in the juices. Add the drained gnocchi, pasta sauce, basil, seasoning and the water and simmer for 5 minutes.
4 Pour the gnocchi mixture into an ovenproof dish and top with the mozzarella slices. Sprinkle with the Parmesan cheese and grill for about 3–4 minutes or until bubbling.

Ideal for a speedy after-work supper, it is perfect served with salad.

Pasta with asparagus, mint pesto & eggs

Serves 2

250g pasta of your choice
250g asparagus spears
4 slices pancetta
1 bunch fresh mint leaves, plus
    extra for sprinkling

100ml good quality olive oil
50g freshly grated Parmesan cheese,
    plus extra for sprinkling
pepper
2 eggs

1 Cook the pasta in a pan of boiling water until al dente or according to the packet instructions. Add the asparagus spears to the boiling pasta water for the last 2–3 minutes of the cooking time.

2 Meanwhile, preheat the grill to medium and grill the pancetta until crisp. Set aside. Put the mint leaves into a food processor with the oil and process to a purée. Stir in the grated Parmesan cheese, lots of pepper and set aside.

3 Poach the eggs in a small pan of barely simmering water for 3–4 minutes.

4 Meanwhile, drain the pasta and asparagus, then mix in the mint pesto. Divide between two serving plates, crumble over the pancetta, sprinkle with extra Parmesan cheese and mint, then lift out the poached egg with a slotted spoon and place on top. Serve immediately.

Quick jambalaya

Illustrated on the following pages

Serves 4

6 pork sausages
2 tbsp olive oil
3 celery sticks, sliced
2 red peppers, seeded and cut into
   small chunks
½ tsp crushed dried chillies

250g wholegrain rice
400g jar crushed tomatoes with
   onion and garlic
425ml hot chicken or vegetable stock
salt and pepper
2 tbsp chopped fresh parsley
   (optional)

1 Preheat the grill to its highest setting. Put the sausages on a baking sheet
and grill for 15–20 minutes, turning once, until brown.
2 Heat the oil in a deep frying pan or wok. Add the celery and peppers and
fry for 2–3 minutes to soften. Add the crushed chillies and the rice and cook,
stirring, for 1 minute, before adding the tomatoes, the hot stock and some
seasoning. Simmer over a medium heat for 20 minutes, stirring occasionally,
until nearly all of the liquid has been absorbed and the rice is tender.
3 When the sausages are cooked, cut them into chunks and stir into the rice.
Sprinkle with parsley and serve with a green salad, if you like.

Courgette, pea & chive risotto

Serves 3
2 tsp olive oil
40g butter
1 small leek, thinly sliced
250g Gallo Risotto Pronto Funghi
  Porcini or regular risotto rice

2 tbsp dry white wine
725ml hot vegetable stock
100g baby courgettes, sliced
100g sugar snap peas, halved
1 heaped tbsp chopped fresh chives

1 Heat the oil and half the butter in a large saucepan. Add the leek and cook for 3–4 minutes over a gentle heat. Stir in the risotto rice. Add the white wine and cook, stirring for 30 seconds.
2 Pour in the hot stock and simmer, stirring occasionally, for 12 minutes, adding the courgettes and sugar snap peas for the final 5 minutes.
3 Stir in the remaining butter and the chives and leave to stand off the heat for 5 minutes before serving.

This is also good served as an accompaniment alongside griddled chicken or baked smoked haddock.

Risotto with sausage & red wine

Serves 4

1.3 litres chicken, beef or veal stock
60g butter
1 large brown onion, chopped
400g Sicilian-style or other good
   quality sausages, meat removed
   from casings

250g risotto rice
120ml robust red wine
handful of fresh flat leaf parsley,
   chopped
60g freshly grated Parmesan cheese
salt and pepper

1 Bring the stock to a gentle simmer in a large saucepan.

2 Meanwhile, heat 40g of the butter in a large, heavy-based saucepan. Add the onion and cook, stirring, over a medium heat for 3 minutes. Increase the heat slightly and add the meat. Cook, stirring, until it colours, breaking up any lumps with a fork. Add the rice and stir gently for 2 minutes. Add the wine, stir, and allow most of the liquid to evaporate.

3 Add the stock, a ladleful at a time, to the rice mixture. Stir frequently and add more stock as it is absorbed. The rice will take 18–25 minutes to cook. When ready it should be soft but retain bite. If the stock runs out before the rice is cooked, continue with simmering water.

4 Remove from the heat and add the parsley, Parmesan cheese and the remaining butter. Season to taste. Cover and allow to rest for 5 minutes before serving.

Smoked haddock & Parma ham risotto

Serves 2
40g butter
4 spring onions, chopped
175g arborio (risotto) rice
570ml hot weak vegetable stock
85g slices Parma ham

100g asparagus spears, cut into 5cm
  lengths
110g smoked haddock, skinned and
  cut into chunks
pepper

1 Melt the butter in a large heavy-based saucepan. Add the spring onions and fry for 2 minutes. Stir in the rice then pour in the stock. Bring to the boil and simmer for 10 minutes, stirring occasionally.
2 Meanwhile, dry-fry the Parma ham slices in a large frying pan until browned on both sides. Set aside to crisp.
3 Add the asparagus to the risotto together with the smoked haddock. Season with pepper and stir for 8–10 minutes or until the rice is tender.
4 Break half the Parma ham into pieces and stir into the risotto then serve topped with the remaining Parma ham.

Chicken with red pepper & noodles

Serves 4

20g fresh mint leaves

4 skinless chicken breast fillets, each about 150g, sliced into thin strips

1 large red pepper, seeded and sliced

small knob of fresh root ginger, peeled and grated

2 garlic cloves, finely chopped

200g sugar snap peas

4 tbsp oyster sauce

1 tbsp vegetable oil

4 tbsp unsalted cashew nuts

600g cooked Chinese or other noodles

1 Chop most of the mint leaves, reserving a few small whole ones for the garnish. Put the chicken strips into a bowl. Add the pepper, ginger, garlic, chopped mint, sugar snap peas and oyster sauce and mix well.

2 Heat the oil in a wok. Add the cashew nuts and cook for 2–3 minutes until golden, then set aside.

3 Add the chicken mixture in two batches to the wok and cook over a high heat for 3–4 minutes, transferring the first batch to a plate while you cook the second, then return everything to the wok, including the noodles and cashew nuts. Heat, tossing together for 5 minutes and serve.

Chicken, prawn & noodle laksa

Serves 2
600g Thai chicken soup
250g medium Thai rice noodles
200g large cooked and peeled
 prawns
squeeze of lime juice, to taste
salt and pepper

To finish
roughly chopped dry-roasted
 peanuts
fresh coriander leaves

1 Pour the soup into a large saucepan and place over a medium heat until just boiling, then lower the heat to a simmer.
2 Add the rice noodles and cook for 2 minutes, stirring occasionally, until the noodles have started to soften. Stir in the prawns and add a squeeze of lime juice to taste. Cook for 1–2 minutes to heat through, then season to taste.
3 Divide the laksa between two deep bowls and sprinkle with some roughly chopped dry-roasted peanuts and coriander leaves to serve.

If Thai chicken soup is unavailable, use fresh cream of chicken soup and add a pinch of dried chilli flakes and a handful of fresh coriander leaves. If you like, add a little piece of chopped lemon grass and galangal.

Beef & vegetable rice noodles

Illustrated on the following pages

Serves 4

250g medium rice noodles

500g thin beef frying steaks

salt and pepper

1 tbsp vegetable oil

1 bunch spring onions, sliced
diagonally

150g bean sprouts

3 medium pak choi, quartered
lengthways

50g dry-roasted peanuts, chopped

3 tbsp dark soy sauce, plus extra
to serve

small handful of fresh coriander
leaves, to garnish

1 Put the noodles in a large flat dish and cover with boiling water. Set aside for 2 minutes to soften, then drain and rinse under cold running water. Leave in cold water to prevent sticking.

2 Season the steaks. Heat a large wok or frying pan, add the steaks and sear for 1–2 minutes, so they are still pink in the middle. Allow to rest for 5 minutes, then slice.

3 Drain the noodles. Heat the oil in the wok and stir-fry the spring onions, bean sprouts and pak choi for 2–3 minutes. Toss in the noodles and most of the peanuts. Drizzle with soy sauce and stir-fry for 1 minute to heat through. Season to taste.

4 Divide the noodles between four bowls. Top with the beef, the remaining peanuts, the coriander leaves and soy sauce.

If you can't get pak choi, use 200g trimmed mangetout, briefly blanched, instead.

Thai-style crab rice noodles

Serves 4

60g stir-fry rice noodles

1 bunch spring onions, trimmed and finely sliced

2 carrots, peeled and cut into very thin strips

100g bean sprouts

5 tbsp sweet chilli sauce

juice of 1 lime

salt and pepper

180g fresh white crabmeat or 170g canned white crabmeat, drained

handful of chopped fresh mint

1 Put the rice noodles into a bowl and cover with boiling water. Set aside until softened. Drain, refresh under cold running water and return the noodles to the bowl.

2 Add the spring onions, carrots and bean sprouts to the noodles. Mix the chilli sauce and lime juice together in another bowl and season. Toss through the noodles with the crabmeat and mint. Divide between four plates and serve.

fast
vegetables, pulses & eggs

Aubergine lasagne

Serves 4

1 large or 2 small aubergines, cut
    into 5mm thick rounds
olive oil cooking spray
700g jar sugocasa with herbs or
    crushed tomatoes with herbs
410g can green lentils, drained and
    rinsed
2 tbsp natural breadcrumbs

For the sauce

40g butter
400g plain flour
500ml milk
salt and pepper

1 Preheat the grill to medium. Spray both sides of the aubergine rounds lightly with oil and place on a grill rack. Grill for 5–7 minutes on both sides until soft.

2 To make the sauce, melt the butter gently, then remove the pan from the heat and add the flour. Gradually whisk in the milk, then return the pan to the heat and whisk until thickened. Season.

3 Meanwhile, pour the tomato sauce and lentils into a saucepan and heat through, stirring once or twice until hot.

4 As soon as the white sauce is ready, alternately layer the tomato sauce, aubergines and white sauce in a 1.75-litre ovenproof dish, ending with a layer of white sauce. Sprinkle with breadcrumbs and grill until the top is golden and crunchy.

Mushroom-stuffed pancakes

Serves 3

25g butter
1 tbsp olive oil
1 small leek, thinly sliced
175g chestnut mushrooms, sliced
125g oyster mushrooms, halved
500g carton ready-made cheese
   sauce
420g ready-made pancakes
20g fresh flat leaf parsley, leaves
   only, chopped
1 tbsp lemon juice
salt and pepper
50g freshly grated Parmesan cheese

1 Preheat the grill to high. Heat the butter and oil in a frying pan. Add the leek and cook for 5 minutes. Add the mushrooms and cook for a further 5–8 minutes or until softened.

2 Meanwhile, warm the cheese sauce in a saucepan or in the microwave. Warm the pancakes for a few minutes in a medium-hot oven or according to the packet instructions. Add the parsley and lemon juice to the mushrooms, season and stir together.

3 Lay out the pancakes and divide the mixture between them, spooning it along one end. Roll them up and place in a warmed, snug-fitting ovenproof dish. Top with the warm sauce and the grated Parmesan cheese and grill for 5 minutes.

Stuffed mushrooms with crumble topping

Makes 4

4 large flat mushrooms
2 tbsp olive oil
1 shallot or small brown onion,
 chopped
1 garlic clove, crushed
75g fresh white breadcrumbs

25g freshly grated Parmesan cheese
1 tbsp chopped fresh chives
1 tbsp chopped fresh parsley
grated zest of ½ lemon
25g butter, melted
salt and pepper
100g goats' cheese log

1 Preheat the oven to 190°C/fan oven 170°C/Gas 5. Remove the stems from the mushrooms and roughly chop. Heat 1 tbsp of the oil in a frying pan over a medium heat and cook the mushroom trimmings, onion and garlic, stirring occasionally, for 4–5 minutes or until the onion is soft. Transfer to a bowl.

2 Add the breadcrumbs, Parmesan cheese, chives, parsley and lemon zest to the bowl and combine. Stir in the melted butter and mix well. Season the mixture well with salt and pepper.

3 Brush the base of the mushrooms with the remaining oil. Slice the goats' cheese log into four thick discs. Top each mushroom with a slice of goats' cheese. Divide the bread mixture between the mushrooms and press down lightly. Transfer the mushrooms to a baking sheet and cook in the oven for 15–20 minutes or until golden and tender.

Spinach & chickpea curry

Serves 2

1 tbsp olive oil
1 onion, sliced
1 large garlic clove, crushed
420g ready-made bhuna sauce or
  other curry sauce
150ml water
100g fine green beans, halved
12 cherry tomatoes, halved
410g can chickpeas, drained and
  rinsed
150g young-leaf spinach
salt and pepper

1 Heat the oil in a large deep-sided frying pan. Add the onion and fry for 8–10 minutes over a medium heat until soft, then add the garlic and cook for a further 1 minute. Add the curry sauce and water and bring to the boil, stirring occasionally.

2 Add the green beans, cherry tomatoes and chickpeas to the pan and simmer, covered, for 10 minutes before adding half the spinach. Cook for a minute or so until the spinach has wilted, then stir in the remaining spinach and, once that has wilted, season to taste and serve.

Serve with warmed naan bread and some lime chutney or pickle.

Stir-fried tofu with summer vegetables

Serves 4
349g silken-style tofu
1½ tbsp sesame seeds
5 tbsp vegetable oil
6 spring onions, thickly sliced on
   the diagonal
250g chestnut mushrooms, halved

200g sugar snap peas, halved
150ml water
2 pak choi, halved
195g jar hoisin and spring onion
   sauce or other Chinese-style sauce

1 Cut the tofu into 2.5cm cubes and pat dry on kitchen paper.
2 Heat a wok or deep-sided frying pan and toast the sesame seeds for a few seconds. Transfer to a bowl. Add the oil to the wok or pan and, when hot, add the tofu. Stir-fry for 6–8 minutes, turning occasionally, until golden. Transfer to a double layer of kitchen paper.
3 Discard all but 1½ tbsp of the oil from the wok or pan and add the spring onions, mushrooms and sugar snap peas. Stir-fry for a minute, then add the water and steam-fry for 1–2 minutes. Add the pak choi and cook for 1 minute then add the tofu, the sauce and the sesame seeds. Toss together for 2 minutes. Serve with cooked basmati rice.

Tofu has been shown to lower cholesterol in the blood. Onions have antibacterial properties and contain flavonoids that provide protection against cardiovascular disease.

Red pepper, olive & tomato tart

Serves 2

375g fresh ready rolled puff pastry
2 tbsp black olive tapenade
185g jar roasted red peppers,
　　drained, reserving some oil, and
　　roughly sliced

125g bocconcini (mini mozzarella
　　balls)
pepper
2 ripe plum tomatoes, quartered
good handful of wild rocket leaves

1 Preheat the oven to 200°C/fan oven 180°C/Gas 6. Cut the puff pastry in half and place on a baking sheet. Freeze the rest.
2 Spread the tapenade over the pastry, leaving a small border all around. Scatter the sliced roasted red peppers over the tart and top with the bocconcini. Season with pepper.
3 Bake for 15 minutes. Top with the plum tomatoes and bake for a further 10 minutes or until the pastry is cooked and golden. Scatter with the wild rocket, drizzle with the reserved oil and cut in half to serve.

Cauliflower & lentil curry

Serves 2

1 small onion, sliced
knob of butter
1 tbsp vegetable oil
200g small cauliflower florets
chopped fresh coriander, plus extra
  to garnish
salt and pepper

For the tarka dhal

500ml water
300g chana lentils or yellow split
  peas
$\frac{1}{2}$ tsp turmeric
1 tbsp melted butter
$\frac{1}{2}$ tsp chilli powder

1 To make the dhal, pour the water into a large pan and add the lentils and turmeric. Bring to the boil over a high heat, skimming any froth that rises to the surface. Lower the heat slightly and simmer fairly rapidly for 45 minutes stirring occasionally, until the lentils are soft and most of the water is absorbed. Combine the melted butter with the chilli powder and stir into the lentils.

2 Meanwhile, put the onion, butter and oil into a bowl, cover with cling film, pierce a few times, then microwave on high (900W) for 5 minutes. Stir and microwave for a further 1–2 minutes, checking constantly, until golden brown. Set aside to cool.

3 Cook the cauliflower florets in a pan of boiling water for about 5 minutes or until tender, then drain and tip into a bowl. Add the dhal, some chopped fresh coriander and a splash of hot water. Gently mix and season to taste.

4 Divide between two plates and top with the onions and some fresh coriander. Serve with cooked basmati rice.

Vegetable bolognese

Serves 4

1 tbsp olive oil
1 red onion, chopped
1 large garlic clove, crushed
100g carrots (about 3), finely sliced
1 red pepper, seeded and chopped
75g mushrooms, chopped

500g carton creamed tomatoes or
   passata
50g broccoli, chopped
handful of fresh basil leaves
250g dried spaghetti
salt

1 Heat the oil in a large pan, add the onion and garlic and fry for a few minutes to soften but not colour. Add the carrots and cook for 5 minutes, then add the pepper and cook for a further 2 minutes. Stir in the mushrooms and tomatoes and bring to the boil. Add the broccoli and basil leaves and simmer for 5 minutes or until all the vegetables are tender.
2 Whiz the vegetables in a food processor, in batches, until very finely chopped. Return the sauce to a saucepan to warm through.
3 Meanwhile, cook the spaghetti in a large pan of boiling salted water for 8–10 minutes or until al dente. Drain and toss through the sauce to serve.

You can make this vegetable sauce in bulk and freeze it, ready for any meal crisis. You can also add this to your regular minced meat bolognese in place of canned tomatoes. Use half the quantity of vegetable sauce to 500g minced meat.

Mushroom, pancetta & spinach pancakes

Serves 2

75g cubed pancetta

150g baby chestnut mushrooms, sliced

2 garlic cloves, crushed

500g ready-made fresh four cheese sauce or other fresh cheese pasta sauce

large handful of baby spinach leaves

4 thin ready-made savoury pancakes

25g Parmesan cheese, freshly grated

salt and pepper

small handful of fresh parsley, roughly chopped

1 Dry-fry the pancetta in a medium-size frying pan for 5 minutes until golden. Add the mushrooms and garlic and cook for a further 3 minutes. Stir in three-quarters of the cheese sauce and heat until just bubbling. Add the spinach and cook for 1 minute until just wilted. Set aside.

2 Preheat the oven to 200°C/fan oven 180°C/Gas 6. Take a pancake and spoon one-quarter of the filling down the centre. Carefully roll the pancake up and put into a baking dish. Repeat with remaining pancakes.

3 Drizzle the remaining cheese sauce over the pancakes, sprinkle with grated Parmesan cheese and season to taste. Bake for 15 minutes until piping hot and turning golden. Scatter over the parsley and serve with plenty of green salad.

Hot Camembert & pepper pastry parcels

Serves 2

425g packet frozen puff pastry,
  thawed
plain flour, for dusting
150g round petit Camembert cheese

4 tbsp cooked mixed peppers
  (from a jar)
pepper
fresh thyme leaves, for sprinkling
1 egg yolk

1 Preheat the oven to 200°C/fan oven 180°C/Gas 6 and put a baking sheet in to heat. Unroll a thawed sheet of puff pastry on a lightly floured surface and cut in half to give two wide rectangles.

2 Cut the Camembert in half to make two semi-circles, then cut each half horizontally to give four semi-circles. Place a piece of cheese in the centre of each pastry rectangle, then top with 1 tbsp of cooked mixed peppers. Rest the remaining cheese on top, season with pepper and sprinkle with some fresh thyme leaves.

3 Beat the egg yolk with a little water in a small bowl. Brush the pastry edges with egg, then bring up the pastry to form a parcel. Press the edges to seal with a fork, then brush each parcel with more egg.

4 Transfer to the hot baking sheet and cook for 20–25 minutes until cooked through and golden. Serve with a green salad.

Warm goats' cheese & red pepper toasties

Serves 4

four 2cm slices ciabatta, cut on the
  diagonal
4 rounded tsp fresh pesto
100g goats' cheese, chilled well, then
  halved lengthways

2 roasted red peppers, from a jar,
  opened out
2 tbsp pine nuts, dry-fried or toasted
  until golden

1 Preheat the grill to its highest setting. Grill the ciabatta slices until golden, then spread with pesto. Put a piece of goats' cheese onto a pepper and roll it up.

2 Repeat with the remaining cheese and pepper, then cut into six 2cm slices per roll. Put three slices onto each piece of ciabatta and grill until beginning to brown. Scatter over the pine nuts and serve with salad leaves.

Rocket pesto-filled mushrooms

Illustrated on the following pages

Serves 2

2 garlic cloves, crushed
25g fresh rocket leaves
5 tbsp extra virgin olive oil
65g fresh white breadcrumbs
salt and pepper

150g Camembert cheese, cut into
  8 slices
1 beef tomato
4 large cup-shaped portobello or
  field mushrooms, stalks removed

1 Put the garlic, rocket and olive oil into a food processor and whiz to give a thick green oil. Add 50g of the breadcrumbs and some seasoning and mix well. Set aside.

2 Heat the oven to 200°C/fan oven 180°C/Gas 6. Cut the tomato into 4 slices. Put a slice into each mushroom then season well. Divide the rocket mixture between each.

3 Lay two slices of Camembert across the mushrooms and transfer to a baking tray. Sprinkle with the remaining breadcrumbs. Bake for 12–15 minutes until the breadcrumbs are lightly golden and the cheese has melted. Serve two mushrooms on each plate with a few dressed salad leaves and plenty of crusty bread.

Mushroom, red wine & thyme ragú

Serves 2

1 tbsp olive oil

1 onion, chopped

200g large flat mushrooms, halved
   and thickly sliced

1 tbsp tomato purée

100ml red wine

100ml hot vegetable stock

few fresh thyme leaves

salt and pepper

home-made mash

1 Heat the oil in a wide saucepan over a medium heat. Add the onion and cook for 5 minutes until softened.

2 Stir in the mushrooms, cover and cook for 5 minutes until the mushrooms have released some juice. Uncover and cook for a few minutes to evaporate the juice then stir in the tomato purée. Cook for 30 seconds then stir in the wine. Let bubble for a few minutes to reduce by half.

3 Stir in the hot stock with a few thyme leaves and let bubble for a few minutes until reduced a little. Season to taste. Spoon over home-made mash, top with more fresh thyme and serve with steamed broccoli.

Quick falafel with harissa dressing

Serves 2–3
410g can chickpeas, drained
3 spring onions, chopped
½ tsp ground cumin
1 tbsp harissa paste
1 lemon
salt and pepper
1 tbsp olive oil

For the dressing
1 tbsp harissa paste
2 tbsp olive oil
1 spring onion, finely chopped

1 Put the chickpeas into a food processor and add the chopped spring onions, ground cumin and harissa paste.
2 Juice ½ a lemon and add 1 tbsp of juice to the chickpeas. Cut the remaining half into wedges to serve and set the remaining juice aside for the dressing. Season and whiz until the mixture comes together. Shape into 6 small, firm patties.
3 Heat the oil in a frying pan over a medium heat. Add the patties and fry for 3–4 minutes on each side until golden.
4 Meanwhile, make the dressing. Mix the harissa paste, oil and some lemon juice to taste together in a bowl. Season to taste and stir in the finely chopped spring onion.
5 Divide the falafels between two or three plates and drizzle with some dressing. Serve with the lemon wedges, some rocket and toasted ciabatta, if you like.

Haloumi & roasted vegetable skewers

Serves 4

50g fresh basil, plus extra to serve

8 tbsp olive oil

salt and pepper

250g haloumi, drained and cubed

1 large red pepper, seeded and
   roughly cubed

6 mushrooms, halved

1 courgette, roughly cubed

2 tbsp pine nuts

400g dried spaghetti

Note: You will also need eight wooden or bamboo skewers.

1 Heat the barbecue. Soak the skewers in cold water for at least 30 minutes.
2 Meanwhile, put the basil, oil and seasoning in a small food processor or
blender and process to a purée. Put 2 tbsp of the mixture into a large bowl.
Add the haloumi and vegetables and gently toss together.
3 Meanwhile, heat a frying pan over a medium heat. Add the pine nuts and
dry-fry for 3–4 minutes, stirring occasionally, until toasted. Set aside.
4 Thread the haloumi and vegetables alternately onto the soaked skewers.
Cook on the hot barbecue for 10 minutes, turning halfway, until the
vegetables are just tender.
5 Meanwhile, cook the spaghetti in a large pan of boiling salted water for
8–10 minutes or until al dente. Drain well, tip back into the pan and toss
with another 2 tbsp of the basil mixture and pine nuts. Divide between four
serving bowls, scatter with basil and serve with the skewers alongside.

To cook indoors: cook the skewers on a
foil-lined baking tray under a hot grill or in
batches in a griddle pan for 10 minutes until
charred. This recipe makes more basil mixture
than you actually need. It keeps for 24 hours,
so toss it through tomato or pasta salads.

Watercress, red onion & rosemary frittata

Illustrated on the following pages

Serves 2
2 tbsp olive oil
knob of butter
1 red onion, sliced
6 eggs

2 tbsp chopped fresh rosemary
salt and pepper
85g watercress, chopped
110g Gruyère cheese, cubed

1 Heat the oil and butter together in a 20cm non-stick frying pan and, when sizzling, add the onion. Cook for 5–7 minutes over a low heat until softened.
2 Preheat the grill to its highest setting. Beat the eggs, rosemary and some seasoning together in a bowl. Scatter the watercress and cheese over the onion and stir together, then pour the egg mixture evenly over the top. Cook for 3–4 minutes or until semi-set but still liquid on top.
3 Place the pan under the grill and cook for a further 3–4 minutes until lightly golden and set. Cut into wedges or squares to serve.

Watercress is one of the best food sources of vitamins C, B1, B6, K and E, iron, calcium, zinc and magnesium, all of which are important for overall health. Rosemary has well-known anti-inflammatory properties, which are believed to have benefits for arthritis and asthma sufferers.

Gorgonzola &
sage omelette

Serves 2

5 eggs, separated
75g Gorgonzola cheese, cut into
   small cubes
1 tsp finely chopped fresh sage
pepper

50g rocket salad
½ small red onion, finely sliced
generous knob of butter
50g sugar snap peas
1 tbsp balsamic vinegar

1 Put the egg yolks into a large bowl and the whites in another. Mix the
yolks with the Gorgonzola, sage and some pepper. Put the rocket into a salad
bowl with the red onion.

2 Heat the butter in a frying pan with a base diameter of 19cm and preheat
the grill to its highest setting. Whisk the egg whites to soft peaks in a large
bowl and fold them into the egg yolk mixture. Pile the mixture into the pan.
Cook over a low heat for 4–5 minutes.

3 Meanwhile, cook the sugar snap peas in a small pan of boiling water
for 3 minutes, drain and toss with the rocket and vinegar.

4 Grill the omelette for 30 seconds and serve immediately with the salad
and some soda bread.

Sweet potato & goats' cheese frittata

Serves 4

1kg sweet potatoes, peeled and cut
   into 2.5cm chunks
salt and pepper
2 tbsp olive oil

1 onion, sliced
6 medium eggs
10g fresh rosemary, leaves chopped
$\frac{1}{2}$ tsp dried crushed chilli flakes
100g goats' cheese, sliced

1 Preheat the grill to high. Bring the potato chunks to the boil in a pan of salted water, cover and simmer for 4–5 minutes or until tender.

2 Meanwhile, heat 1 tbsp of the oil in a 20cm ovenproof non-stick frying pan and gently cook the onion. Drain the potatoes, add to the onion with the remaining oil and cook for 3 minutes.

3 Whisk the eggs, rosemary and chilli flakes together in a bowl, season, then pour over the potato mixture. Cook over a low heat, tilting the pan occasionally, and drawing in the sides of the mixture so the egg cooks evenly. When cooked around the sides and on the base, about 5 minutes, remove from the heat.

4 Arrange the slices of goats' cheese on top, then grill for about 4 minutes until it starts to melt and the top is set. Serve with a crunchy green salad and chutney.

Roast vegetable, goats' cheese & lentil salad

Serves 4

1 courgette, cut into 4cm cubes
1 aubergine, cut into 4cm cubes
1 red pepper, cut into strips
1 yellow pepper, cut into strips
4 fat garlic cloves, unpeeled
$\frac{1}{2}$ tsp ground cumin
$\frac{1}{2}$ tsp ground coriander
4 tbsp olive oil

salt and pepper
200g green lentils, such as Puy
  lentils
1 bay leaf
50g young-leaf spinach
juice of $\frac{1}{2}$ lemon
100g goats' cheese
2 tbsp roughly chopped fresh mint

1 Preheat the oven to 200°C/fan oven 180°C/Gas 6. Place the prepared vegetables in a large roasting tray. Bruise the unpeeled garlic cloves with the back of a knife and add to the tray with the spices and 2 tbsp of the oil.
2 Season well and mix to coat the vegetables in the oil. Cover with foil and roast on a high shelf for 30–40 minutes or until tender. Remove from the oven, set aside one of the garlic cloves and leave to cool.
3 Meanwhile, cook the lentils with the bay leaf in a large pan of boiling water for 15–20 minutes or according to the packet instructions until tender. Drain, season, then leave to cool.
4 Toss the vegetables, lentils and spinach in a large serving bowl. Mash the reserved garlic clove into the pan juices. Add the lemon juice and the remaining oil to the roasting tin, mix and season very well. Pour over the salad, toss well and check the seasoning. Crumble the goats' cheese on top and scatter over the fresh mint.

Mushroom, tomato & egg burger

Serves 2
2 large flat mushrooms
2 thick slices beef tomato
garlic butter
2 eggs
2 burger buns
few baby spinach leaves

1 Preheat the grill to medium. Destalk the mushrooms and put on a grill pan or baking tray, together with the tomato slices. Dot everything with about 1 tbsp of garlic butter and cook under the grill for 5 minutes until tender.
2 Meanwhile, heat a small knob of garlic butter in a frying pan. Crack in the eggs and cook for a few minutes to set the white.
3 Toast the burger buns. Top each bottom half with a few baby spinach leaves, a grilled mushroom, a tomato slice and a fried egg. Sandwich with the bun tops and serve with oven-baked chips.

Smoked salmon & courgette omelette

Serves 2
4 large eggs
2 tsp water
1 courgette, grated
handful of fresh chives, chopped,
    plus extra to garnish

salt and pepper
1 tbsp butter
50g smoked salmon trimmings

1 Beat the eggs in a bowl with the water. Mix in the grated courgette, chopped chives and salt and pepper.
2 Melt a little butter in a small, non-stick frying pan. When hot, add half the egg mixture and cook for 1 minute, stirring until the egg is beginning to set in places. Scatter evenly with the smoked salmon and cook for a further 1–2 minutes until the egg is golden underneath, and just set on top.
3 Slide the omelette out onto a serving plate, folding it over as you go. Repeat. Scatter a few chopped chives over each omelette and serve with a crisp, green salad.

fast
puddings

Chocolate, mango & passion fruit pots

Serves 4

1 large mango
2 chocolate muffins, cut into chunks
2 passion fruit
142ml carton whipping cream

2 heaped tbsp Greek yogurt
1 level tbsp caster sugar, or to taste
2 level tsp soft brown sugar
½ tsp ground cinnamon

1 Slice the 'cheek' off either side of the mango stone. Score the flesh lengthways, then crossways, into a grid pattern. Push the mango skin inside out and cut away the flesh into cubes.
2 Layer the chunks of muffin with the mango in four tumblers or glass trifle bowls, then spoon the passion fruit on top.
3 Whip the cream until lightly thickened, then fold in the yogurt and caster sugar to taste. Peak a heaped tbsp of the cream mix on top of each dessert.
4 Mix the soft brown sugar and cinnamon together in a small bowl and sprinkle over the top.

Low-fat yogurt & apricot pots

Serves 4
250g dried apricots, halved
150ml freshly squeezed orange juice
150ml carton Greek yogurt
25g pistachio nuts, chopped
4 tsp Greek honey, for drizzling

1 Place the dried apricots in a small saucepan with the freshly squeezed orange juice and simmer for 10 minutes. Leave to cool then divide the fruit, including the juice, between four tumblers or ramekins.
2 Top each one with the Greek yogurt, then scatter the pistachios over the top. To finish, drizzle with Greek honey.

Rhubarb & ginger fool

Serves 6

570g rhubarb, cut into 2.5cm pieces
95g golden caster sugar, plus extra
　to taste
2 pieces stem ginger, thinly sliced,
　plus 2 tbsp of the syrup

500ml fresh custard or equivalent of
　homemade thick custard, cooled
142ml carton double cream

1 Put the rhubarb and sugar in a saucepan. Cover and simmer over a low heat until softened, adding more sugar if the rhubarb is still tart.
2 Put half of the fruit into a large bowl. Stir the stem ginger syrup into the remaining rhubarb and leave to cool for 10 minutes, then spoon into the bottom of six 225ml glasses.
3 Pour the custard into the bowl with the rhubarb and stir well to combine. When completely cool, whip the cream in another bowl and mix into the rhubarb-and-custard mixture until combined. Pour into the glasses and top with the stem ginger slices.

Strawberry & passion fruit salad

Serves 6

454g strawberries, hulled and sliced
  in half
2 oranges, one peeled and
  segmented, the other juiced

4 passion fruits
2 tbsp orange blossom water
2 tbsp caster or light brown soft
  sugar
2 tbsp shelled pistachio nuts

1 Put the strawberries in a serving bowl with the orange segments.
2 Cut the passion fruits in half and, using a teaspoon, scoop the seeds into a jug. Add the orange juice, orange blossom water and sugar to the jug and stir until all the sugar has dissolved. Pour over the salad and leave to chill until required.
3 Serve at room temperature, sprinkling the pistachio nuts over the top just before serving.

Raspberry, sherry & nut trifle

Illustrated on the following pages

Serves 6

250g amaretti biscuits

4 tbsp sweet sherry

150g raspberries, plus extra to
decorate

icing sugar, to taste

500g ready-made crème anglaise or
vanilla custard

284ml carton double cream, whipped

To decorate

chopped toasted hazelnuts

fresh mint leaves

1 Put the amaretti biscuits into the bottom of a large glass bowl and sprinkle well with sweet sherry.

2 Use a fork to crush the 150g raspberries with icing sugar to taste, then spoon over the soaked biscuits. Add a few more whole raspberries.

3 Spoon over the crème anglaise or vanilla custard and top with plenty of whipped fresh double cream. Decorate with whole raspberries, chopped toasted hazelnuts and mint leaves.

Cherries jubilee

Serves 4
100ml water
1 tbsp arrowroot
150ml crème de cassis
grated zest and juice of 1 orange
500g whole cherries, stalks removed
500g vanilla ice cream

1 Mix 1 tbsp of the water with the arrowroot to form a paste. Add the rest of
the water to a pan with the cassis, orange zest and juice. Bring to the boil
and stir in the paste. Stir until thick and clear.
2 Add the cherries and heat for 3 minutes. Scoop the ice cream into bowls
and spoon over the sauce.

Arrowroot thickens the sauce without
cloudiness, but you can use cornflour instead.

Tiramisu

Serves 4

2 tsp espresso coffee powder
50ml boiling water
1 tbsp coffee liqueur
3 tbsp maple syrup

250g tub quark
$\frac{1}{2}$ tsp vanilla extract
100g fat-free vanilla yogurt
10 sponge fingers
cocoa powder, for dusting

1 Stir the coffee into the boiling water in a bowl, then leave to cool. Stir in the liqueur and 1 tbsp maple syrup.
2 Beat the quark, vanilla extract and remaining maple syrup together in another bowl until smooth. Stir in the yogurt.
3 Break the sponge fingers in half. Dip two pieces briefly into the coffee syrup and put in a wine glass or a shallow dessert glass. Repeat with three more glasses. Spoon over some of the quark mixture, then repeat the layers with the remaining ingredients, using three sponge finger halves per glass for the second layer. Place the glasses on a tray and chill for 1 hour.
4 Dust the desserts with a little cocoa powder to serve.

Limoncello syllabub with lemon sugar

Makes 10

125g raspberries
50ml limoncello, plus extra for
  topping up
finely grated zest of 2 lemons
50g golden caster sugar
284ml carton double cream
2 tbsp Greek yogurt

1 Divide the raspberries between 10 shot glasses, topping each with a little of the extra limoncello.
2 Grind the lemon zest with 3 tbsp of the caster sugar in a pestle and mortar until fine.
3 Whip the cream and 50ml limoncello together in a large bowl until soft peaks form. Add half the zest mixture and the remaining sugar then fold in with the Greek yogurt. Spoon the cream over the raspberries and sprinkle with the remaining lemon sugar to serve.

Limoncello is an Italian lemon liqueur best served straight from the freezer. Find it in off-licences, Italian delis and some larger supermarkets.

Chocolate-coated strawberries

Serves 2
50g plain chocolate, chopped
6 strawberries

1 Melt the chopped chocolate in a bowl set over a pan of simmering water or microwave for 30 seconds until smooth.
2 Dip the bottom half of the strawberries into the chocolate and place on a baking sheet lined with baking paper. Chill for about 15 minutes until the chocolate is set then serve.

Toffee banana trifles

Serves 6

6 slices bought chocolate cake

6 tbsp Baileys

3 medium bananas

6 tbsp dulce de leche toffee sauce or
   other toffee or caramel sauce

500g ready-made fresh custard

142ml carton double cream

splash of vanilla extract

edible small gold or silver balls, to
   decorate

1 To prepare, break up the chocolate cake into pieces and divide between six dessert glasses. Drizzle 1 tbsp Baileys over each. Slice the bananas and divide the slices between the glasses. Dollop a spoonful of toffee sauce over each, followed by a few spoonfuls of custard. Chill until required.

2 To serve, whip the double cream and vanilla extract together in a bowl until thick. Spoon into each glass and decorate the top with edible gold or silver balls.

Microwaved chocolate pots

Serves 6
300g plain dark chocolate,
   broken into chunks
500g fromage frais

1 Put the chocolate pieces into a bowl and microwave on medium (500W) for 2–3 minutes, then stir until smooth.
2 Add the fromage frais and stir. Divide the mixture between six individual ramekins or pots and eat straightaway.

You can chill these pots overnight but they have a silky smooth texture if eaten at once.

Iced pineapple
& mango slush

Serves 6

2 ripe mangoes
1 fresh pineapple
6 scoops vanilla ice cream, to serve

1 Peel and stone the mangoes and cut away all the flesh. Roughly chop the flesh, put into a food processor and process to a smooth purée. Spoon the purée into a freezerproof container and freeze for $1\frac{1}{2}$ hours until slushy.
2 Peel and core the pineapple, then cut the flesh into small cubes. Stir the pineapple into the mango and return to the freezer.
3 Spoon the semi-frozen mango and pineapple mixture into a container and close tightly. Spoon some iced pineapple and mango slush into six pretty paper cups or plastic tumblers and put a scoop of vanilla ice cream on top. Serve immediately.

You can eat this on its own or, better still, take it to the beach in an ice-cold flask and buy some vanilla ice cream to eat with it. To make sure the pineapple and mango slush stays extra cold, pre-chill the flask first by filling with ice and leaving it for a few hours. Tip out the ice before adding the slush.

Apple & ginger yogurt pots

Serves 2
50g ginger biscuits (about 5)
1 Golden Delicious apple
1 tbsp lemon juice
½ tsp caster sugar
150ml natural yogurt

1 Place the biscuits in a plastic food bag and bash with a rolling pin to crush. Divide two-thirds between two glasses or tumblers and set aside.
2 Grate the apple into a bowl and stir in the lemon juice to prevent it from discolouring. Sprinkle with the sugar then divide between the glasses.
3 Top with the yogurt and sprinkle with the remaining ginger biscuit crumbs. Serve immediately or cover and chill for up to 2 hours.

If you reach for yogurt after a meal, try adding grated apple and crushed biscuits for something a bit special.

Plums roasted with sloe gin

Serves 4
12 plums, halved and stoned
150ml sloe gin (see recipe, below) or
  use shop-bought sloe gin
juice of 1 orange, plus a little extra
60g golden caster sugar

For the sloe gin
450g sloes, washed
450g sugar
70cl bottle gin

1 Prick the sloes with a fork and combine in a large Kilner jar with the sugar and gin.

2 Turn the jar every day for the first week or so to dissolve the sugar and colour the gin evenly.

3 When the sloe gin is ready, preheat the oven to 200°C/fan oven 180°C/Gas 6. Put the plums, cut-side up, in a large roasting tin. Mix the gin and orange juice together and pour over the fruit. Sprinkle with the sugar and bake for 15–20 minutes until tender.

4 Using a slotted spoon, transfer to a large dish to cool. Put the roasting tin over a high heat on the hob. Bring to the boil and cook for 3–4 minutes or until reduced and syrupy. Leave to cool, then pour over the cooled plums. Serve with shortbread and ice cream or clotted cream.

Making your own sloe gin is easy. Keep for at least 3 months before serving – ideally, pick the sloes in September and the gin will ready to drink at Christmas.

Buttermilk pancakes with honeyed bananas

Illustrated on the following pages

Serves 4–6

200g plain flour
$\frac{1}{2}$ tsp bicarbonate of soda
25g caster sugar
2 eggs, lightly beaten
284ml carton buttermilk or milk
2–3 tbsp milk, if needed

50g butter, for frying
6 tbsp runny honey
finely grated zest and juice of
  1 orange
4 bananas, thickly sliced
200g Greek yogurt, to serve

1 Sift the plain flour, bicarbonate of soda and caster sugar together in a large bowl and make a well in the centre. Pour in the eggs and buttermilk, then gradually whisk in the flour mixture until you have a perfectly smooth batter. Add the milk if the batter seems a little thick.

2 Heat one-quarter of the butter in a large, non-stick frying pan over a medium heat. Add four large spoonfuls of the pancake batter, spaced apart, to make 9cm round pancakes. Cook for 2 minutes, until golden underneath, then flip over and cook for a further 2 minutes until cooked through. Remove, keep warm in a low oven and repeat with the remaining batter to make about 16 pancakes in total.

3 Put the honey, orange zest and juice in the frying pan and boil for 3 minutes until thick and syrupy. Add the bananas and cook for a further 30 seconds. Remove from the heat, spoon the syrup over the pancakes and serve with spoonfuls of Greek yogurt.

If buttermilk is unavailable, then use ordinary milk instead.

Crêpes Suzette

Makes 4 large or 8 medium pancakes
125g plain flour
pinch of salt
1 medium egg, beaten
1 tsp icing sugar
½ orange zest, grated
275–300ml semi-skimmed milk
vegetable or sunflower oil, for frying

For the sauce
40g caster sugar
40g butter
juice of 2 small oranges
2 tbsp Cointreau
2 tbsp brandy

To finish
thin strips of orange zest
crème fraîche (optional)

1 Sift the flour with the salt into a large bowl. Make a well in the centre, pour in the egg, add the icing sugar and the grated orange zest. Slowly whisk in enough of the milk until you have a smooth batter – the consistency of pouring cream. Set aside to rest for at least 20 minutes.
2 Heat about a 28cm crêpe pan or heavy-based frying pan over a medium heat. When hot, dip some kitchen paper in the oil and wipe a thin layer across the surface of the pan. Add a small ladleful of batter and tilt the pan to swirl the batter evenly and thinly across the base. Cook for 1–2 minutes until the pancake is golden underneath.
3 Loosen all around the pancake with a palette knife. Flip over and cook for a further minute until golden. Slide out onto a plate and repeat to finish up the batter. Oil the pan between each pancake. Fold the pancakes into eighths or quarters, depending on their size and set aside on serving plates.
4 Make the sauce by slowly dissolving the caster sugar in a frying pan. Increase the heat and cook until golden. Add the butter and the orange juice and cook until the sauce is simmering. Stir in the Cointreau, then pour over the brandy and flambé by carefully igniting the sauce with a long taper. Remove from the heat while the flames die down, drizzle the pancakes with the orange sauce. Scatter with thin strips of orange zest and serve with a dollop of crème fraîche, if you like.

Apple pancakes with toffee sauce & yogurt

Illustrated on the following pages

Serves 4–6
50g butter
225g self-raising flour
2 tsp baking powder
50g caster sugar
175ml buttermilk or milk
2 medium eggs
175ml full-cream milk
500g cooking apples

1 tsp vanilla extract
Greek-style yogurt, to serve

For the toffee sauce
50g unsalted butter
50g light muscovado sugar
2 tbsp golden syrup
2 tbsp double cream

1 To make the toffee sauce, put the butter, sugar and golden syrup into a small pan and bring slowly to the boil, stirring. Lower the heat and simmer for 3 minutes until thick. Stir in the cream, then set aside to cool.
2 Make clarified butter by melting the butter in a pan. Remove from the heat and leave to stand for a few minutes. Pour off the clear butter into a bowl and set aside. Discard the milky-white solids at the bottom of the pan.
3 Sift the flour, baking powder and sugar into a bowl, make a well in the centre, then add the buttermilk, eggs and milk. Whisk until smooth and thick. Peel, core and coarsely grate the apples and measure out 300g. Stir into the batter with the vanilla.
4 Heat a large, non-stick frying pan over a medium heat. Brush the base with a little clarified butter. Add four large spoonfuls of the batter, spaced well apart, and cook for 2 minutes until bubbles appear on top of the pancakes and they are golden brown underneath. Flip and cook for 1 minute. Transfer to a plate and keep warm while you cook the rest, to make about 16.
5 Pile the pancakes onto warmed plates, top with a large spoonful of yogurt and drizzle with the toffee sauce. Serve immediately.

Apples discolour quickly when peeled, so drop the pieces into lightly acidulated water (water and lemon juice) as you go.

Acknowledgements

Most of the recipes in this book were first published in **delicious.** magazine or **Sainsbury's Magazine**. We are thankful to all the staff (past and present) involved in both magazines and to those at the Seven Publishing Group for providing the material and their assistance.

Recipes by:

Felicity Barnum Bob
Red pepper & goats' cheese toasted panini p16, Salmon fishfingers p135, Vegetable bolognese p221, Cherries jubilee p261, Microwaved chocolate pots p270

Kate Belcher
Parma ham & smoked mozzarella pizza p23, Pea, lettuce & tarragon soup p29, Chilled avocado soup with zingy salsa p33, Summery Spanish-style soup p39, Beef steak chilli con carne p61, Jerk pork steaks with fruity salsa p73, Pork & apple burgers with blue cheese p74, Pork chops with prunes & crème fraîche p78, Spiced lamb with apricots p81, Indonesian-style chicken couscous p96, Honeyed duck & vegetable stir-fry p102, Duck with fig, pine nut & mint couscous p103, Prawns with mango & avocado p112, Mussels with wine & basil tomatoes p115, Smoked mackerel & chorizo potatoes p120, Green bean, tomato, spinach & Feta pasta p178, Olive, chorizo & tomato pasta p181,

Beef & vegetable rice noodles p197, Red pepper, olive & tomato tart p217, Cauliflower & lentil curry p218, Mushroom, pancetta & spinach pancakes p222, Hot Camembert & pepper pastry parcels p225, Quick falafel with harissa dressing p233, Haloumi & roasted vegetable skewers p234, Smoked salmon & courgette omelette p245, Crêpes Suzette p280

Lorna Brash
Kedgeree p127

Geli Carney
Strawberry & passion fruit salad p256

Matthew Drennan
Sausage pittas with caramelised onions p19, Tomato, sausage & Emmental croissants p26, Tomato & goats' cheese tarts p37, Chicken, pasta & butter bean ramen p48, Peppered steak with a rich shallot sauce p59, Pork kebabs on minted broad beans with Feta p77, Quick Thai green chicken curry p99, Sweet-&-sour prawns with lime p111, Thai-poached salmon p136, Tortellini with lemon & courgette p177, Pasta with asparagus, mint pesto & eggs p184, Chicken, prawn & noodle laksa p196, Thai-style crab rice noodles p200, Rocket pesto-filled mushrooms p227, Mushroom, red wine & thyme ragú p230, Mushroom, tomato & egg burger p243, Raspberry, sherry & nut trifle p257,

Chocolate-coated strawberries p266, Toffee banana trifles p269, Iced pineapple & mango slush p273

Brian Glover
Egg with mustard mayo & cress p43

Silvana Franco
Spiced & buttered crab p45

David Herbert
Risotto with sausage & red wine p191, Stuffed mushrooms with crumble topping p210

Catherine Hill
Mussels in a coconut & lemon grass broth p51, Buttermilk pancakes with honeyed bananas p277

Ghillie James
Runner bean salad with Feta cheese p38, Stir-fried kale with beef & black bean sauce p62, Hot crab ramekins p126, Smoked haddock & Parma ham risotto p192, Warm goats' cheese & red pepper toasties p226, Roast vegetable, goats' cheese & lentil salad p242, Chocolate, mango & passion fruit pots p250, Rhubarb & ginger fool p254

Debbie Major
Grilled flat fish with herb & caper dressing p143, Pan-fried fish fillets with crispy bacon p144, Crab linguine with chilli, lemon & garlic p171, Tiramisu p262, Apple pancakes with toffee sauce & yogurt p281

David Morgan
Limoncello syllabub with lemon sugar p265

Kim Morphew
Cheat's beef stroganoff p58, Linguine with a fresh tomato & olive sauce p167

Tom Norrington-Davies
Clams with pea shoots & wild garlic p114, Plums roasted with sloe gin p276

Sarah Randell
Chargrilled mackerel with balsamic tomatoes p121

Sarah Randell & Ghillie James
Smart beans on toast p22, Tuscan bean soup with rosemary & pesto p30, Toasted muffins with smoked salmon p44, Chilli squid salad with peanuts, Cajun beef wraps p56, Pork, pesto & mozzarella parcels p63, Pork fillet with mushrooms & beans p69, Pork with spinach, raisins & pine nuts p70, Lamb chops with fennel & courgettes p82, Mustard & herb-crumbed lamb p84, Lamb patties with tzatziki p85, Chicken breasts with tarragon & tagliatelle p88, Chicken, ham & mustard pot pies p91,

Chicken with lime, honey & chilli p92, Moroccan chicken with prunes & lemon p95, Chilli squid salad with peanuts p108, Fish & chips with herby dip p119, Mackerel, tomato & mustard tart p124, Smoked haddock with Florentine sauce p131, Roast spiced cod with mango & lime p132, Plaice with mushrooms & Parmesan p139, Steamed hoki with lime, chilli & ginger p140, Boccoletti with prawns, peas & beans p150, Conchiglie with haddock & broccoli p153, Penne with pancetta, mozzarella & basil p154, Penne with artichokes, goats' cheese & olives p157, Penne with sausage, fennel & garlic p158, Orechiette with chicken & artichokes p162, Pasta bake with sausage & spinach p163, Linguine with asparagus & pancetta p168, Linguine with leeks, bacon, ciabatta & chilli p170, Ravioli with butternut, sage & pine nuts p174, Gnocchi with peppers, spinach & mozzarella p182, Quick jambalaya p185, Courgette, pea & chive risotto p188,

Chicken with red pepper & noodles p195, Aubergine lasagne p206, Mushroom-stuffed pancakes p209, Spinach & chickpea curry p213, Stir-fried tofu with summer vegetables p214, Watercress, red onion & rosemary frittata p235, Gorgonzola & sage omelette p239, Sweet potato & goats' cheese frittata p240

Gillian Rhys
Grilled crottin wrapped in prosciutto p34

Annie Rigg
Chorizo roasted pepper & rocket sandwich p15, Mozzarella, figs & Parma ham bruschetta p20

Natalie Seldon
Chicken & aubergine melts p12

Harriet Staveley
Gammon steaks with mustard & cider sauce p66, Low-fat yogurt & apricot pots p253

Mitzie Wilson
Apple & ginger yogurt pots p274

Photography credits
Steve Baxter 2, 10–11, 18, 24–5, 32, 46–7, 106-7, 110, 113, 122–3, 215, 236–7, 264, 272, 275, 278–9, 282–3; Alan Benson 190; Peter Cassidy 7, 50, 64–5, 83, 90, 130, 141, 156, 176, 183, 186–7, 194, 211; Jean Cazals 93, 138, 152, 159, 212, 238, 267; Stephen Conroy 268; Jonathan Gregson 263; Will Heap 252, 255; Janine Hosegood 27, 36, 228–9; Richard Jung 28, 31, 57, 68, 71, 86–7, 89, 94, 109, 125, 133, 148–9, 155, 169, 189, 204–5, 207, 208, 241; Veronique Le Plat 17; Andrew Montgomery 128–9; Gareth Morgans 97, 98, 118, 166, 232, 251; Lis Parsons 13, 72, 75, 100–1, 134, 151, 160–1, 164–5, 175, 179, 193, 198–9, 220, 248–9, 260, 271; Michael Paul 42, 142, 145, 172–3; Deirdre Rooney 54–5, 76, 137, 201; Clive Streeter 40–1, 223; Peter Thiedeke 1, 49, 60, 79, 80, 116–7, 180, 216, 219, 224, 231, 244, 258–9; Simon Walton 14, 21; Philip Webb 35, 67.

A

Apple & ginger yogurt pots 274
Apple pancakes with toffee
  sauce & yogurt 281
apricots, dried
  Low-fat yogurt & apricot pots
    253
artichokes
  Orechiette with chicken &
    artichokes 162
  Penne with artichokes, goats'
    cheese & olives 157
asparagus
  Linguine with asparagus &
    pancetta 168
  Pasta with asparagus, mint
    pesto & eggs 184
aubergines
  Aubergine lasagne 206
  Chicken & aubergine melts 12
avocados
  Chilled avocado soup with
    zingy salsa 33
  Prawns with mango &
    avocado 112

B

bananas
  Buttermilk pancakes with
    honeyed bananas 277
  Toffee banana trifles 269
beans
  Green bean, tomato, spinach
    & feta pasta 178
  Runner bean salad with Feta
    cheese 38
  see also butter beans;
    cannellini
beef
  Beef & vegetable rice noodles
    197
  Beef steak chilli con carne 61
  Cajun beef wraps 56
  Cheat's beef stroganoff 58
  Peppered steak with a rich
    shallot sauce 59
  Stir-fried kale with beef &
    black bean sauce 62
Boccoletti with prawns, peas
  & beans 150
butter beans
  Chicken, pasta & butter bean
    ramen 48
  Smart beans on toast 22
Buttermilk pancakes with
  honeyed bananas 277
butternut squash
  Ravioli with butternut, sage
    & pine nuts 174

C

Cajun beef wraps 56
Camembert & pepper pastry
  parcels 225
cannellini
  Tuscan bean soup with
    rosemary & pesto 30
  see also Smart beans on toast
Cauliflower & lentil curry 218
Cheat's beef stroganoff 58
Cherries jubilee 261
chicken
  Chicken & aubergine melts 12
  Chicken breasts with
    tarragon & tagliatelle 88
  Chicken, ham & mustard pot
    pies 91
  Chicken, pasta & butter bean
    ramen 48
  Chicken, prawn & noodle
    laksa 196
  Chicken with lime, honey &
    chilli 92
  Chicken with red pepper &
    noodles 195
  Indonesian-style chicken
    couscous 96
  Moroccan chicken with
    prunes & lemon 95
  Orechiette with chicken &
    artichokes 162
  Quick Thai green chicken
    curry 99
  see also Honeyed duck &
    vegetable stir-fry
chickpeas
  Quick falafel with harissa
    dressing 233
  Spinach & chickpea curry 213
Chilli squid salad with peanuts
  108
chocolate
  Chocolate-coated strawberries
    266
  Chocolate, mango & passion
    fruit pots 250
  Microwaved chocolate pots
    270
chorizo
  Chorizo, roasted pepper &
    rocket sandwich 15
  Olive, chorizo & tomato pasta
    181
  Smart beans on toast 22
  Smoked mackerel & chorizo
    potatoes 120
Clams with pea shoots & wild
  garlic 114

cod
  Roast spiced cod with mango
    & lime 132
Conchiglie with haddock
    broccoli 153
courgettes
  Courgette, pea & chive risotto
    188
  Smoked salmon & courgette
    omelette 245
  Tortellini with lemon &
    courgette 177
couscous
  Duck with fig, pine nut &
    mint couscous 103
  Indonesian-style chicken
    couscous 96
crab
  Crab linguine with chilli,
    lemon & garlic 171
  Hot crab ramekins 126
  Spiced & buttered crab 45
  Thai-style crab rice noodles 200
Crêpes Suzette 280
curries
  Cauliflower & lentil 218
  Quick Thai green chicken 99
  Spinach & chickpea 213

D

duck
  Duck with fig, pine nut &
    mint couscous 103
  Honeyed duck & vegetable
    stir-fry 102

E

eggs
  Egg with mustard mayo &
    cress 43
  Mushroom, tomato &
    egg burger 243
  see also omelettes; pancakes

F

Falafel with harissa dressing,
  Quick 233
flounder
  Grilled flat fish with herb &
    caper dressing 143
  Pan-fried fish fillets with
    crispy bacon 144
frittata 235, 240

G

Gammon steaks with mustard
  & cider sauce 66
Gnocchi with peppers, spinach
  & mozzarella 182

goats' cheese
  Grilled crottin wrapped in prosciutto 34
  Red pepper & goats' cheese toasted panini 16
  Sweet potato & goats' cheese frittata 240
  Tomato & goats' cheese tarts 37
  Warm goats' cheese & red pepper toasties 226
Gorgonzola & sage omelette 239

H

haddock, smoked
  Conchiglie with haddock & broccoli 153
  Kedgeree 127
  Smoked haddock & Parma ham risotto 192
  Smoked haddock with Florentine sauce 131
Haloumi & roasted vegetable skewers 234
Hoki with lime, chilli & ginger, Steamed 140
Honeyed duck & vegetable stir-fry 102

I

Iced pineapple & mango slush 273
Indonesian-style chicken couscous 96

J

Jambalaya, Quick 185
Jerk pork steaks with fruity salsa 73

K

Kale with beef & black bean sauce, Stir-fried 62

L

lamb
  Lamb chops with fennel & courgettes 82
  Lamb patties with tzatziki 85
  Mustard & herb-crumbed lamb 84
  Spiced lamb with apricots 81
Lasagne, Aubergine 206
lentils
  Cauliflower & lentil curry 218
Limoncello syllabub with lemon sugar 265

linguine
  Crab linguine with chilli, lemon & garlic 171
  Linguine with asparagus & pancetta 168
  Linguine with a fresh tomato & olive sauce 167
  Linguine with leeks, bacon, ciabatta & chilli 170

M

mackerel
  Chargrilled mackerel with balsamic tomatoes 121
mackerel, smoked
  Mackerel, tomato & mustard tart 124
  Smoked mackerel & chorizo potatoes 120
mangoes
  Chocolate, mango & passion fruit pots 250
  Iced pineapple & mango slush 273
  Prawns with mango avocado 112
megrim see flounder
Microwaved chocolate pots 270
Moroccan chicken with prunes & lemon 95
Mozzarella, figs & Parma ham bruschetta 20
Muffins with smoked salmon, Toasted 44
mushrooms
  Mushroom, pancetta & spinach pancakes 222
  Mushroom, red wine & thyme ragú 230
  Mushroom-stuffed pancakes 209
  Mushroom, tomato & egg burger 243
  Rocket pesto-filled mushrooms 227
  Stuffed mushrooms with crumble topping 210
Mussels in a coconut & lemon grass broth 51
Mussels with wine & basil tomatoes 115

O

Olive, chorizo & tomato pasta 181
omelettes
  Gorgonzola & sage 239
  Smoked salmon & courgette 245

Orechiette with chicken & artichokes 162

P

pancakes 209, 222, 277, 281
pancetta
  Linguine with asparagus & pancetta 168
  Mushroom, pancetta & spinach pancakes 222
  Penne with pancetta, mozzarella & basil 154
Parma ham & smoked mozzarella pizza 23
passion fruit
  Chocolate, mango & passion fruit pots 250
  Strawberry & passion fruit salad 256
pasta
  Boccoletti with prawns, peas & beans 150
  Conchiglie with haddock & broccoli 153
  Green bean, tomato, spinach & feta pasta 178
  Olive, chorizo & tomato pasta 181
  Orechiette with chicken & artichokes 162
  Pasta bake with sausage & spinach 163
  Pasta with asparagus, mint pesto & eggs 184
  Ravioli with butternut, sage & pine nuts 174
  Tortellini with lemon & courgette 177
  see also linguine; penne
Pea, lettuce & tarragon soup 29
penne
  Penne with artichokes, goats' cheese & olives 157
  Penne with pancetta, mozzarella & basil 154
  Penne with sausage, fennel & garlic 158
  see also Boccoletti with prawns, peas & beans
Peppered steak with a rich shallot sauce 59
peppers
  Chicken with red pepper & noodles 195
  Chorizo, roasted pepper & rocket sandwich 15
  Gnocchi with peppers, spinach & mozzarella 182

Red pepper & goats' cheese toasted panini 16
Red pepper, olive & tomato tart 217
Warm goats' cheese & red pepper toasties 226
Pineapple & mango slush, Iced 273
plaice
  Grilled flat fish with herb & caper dressing 143
  Pan-fried fish fillets with crispy bacon 144
  Plaice with mushrooms & Parmesan 139
Plums roasted with sloe gin 276
pork
  Jerk pork steaks with fruity salsa 73
  Pork & apple burgers with blue cheese 74
  Pork chops with prunes & crème fraîche 78
  Pork fillet with mushrooms & beans 69
  Pork kebabs on minted broad beans with Feta 77
  Pork, pesto & mozzarella parcels 63
  Pork with spinach, raisins & pine nuts 70
prawns
  Boccoletti with prawns, peas & beans 150
  Prawns with mango avocado 112
  Sweet-and-sour prawns with lime 111

R
Raspberry, sherry & nut trifle 257
Ravioli with butternut, sage & pine nuts 174
Rhubarb & ginger fool 254
risotti
  Courgette, pea & chive risotto 188
  Risotto with sausage & red wine 191
  Smoked haddock & Parma ham risotto 192
Rocket pesto-filled mushrooms 227

S
salads
  Chilli squid salad with peanuts 108

Roast vegetable, goats' cheese & lentil salad 242
Runner bean salad with Feta cheese 38
salmon
  Salmon fishfingers 135
  Thai-poached salmon 136
salmon, smoked
  Smoked salmon & courgette omelette 245
  Toasted muffins with smoked salmon 44
sausages
  Pasta bake with sausage & spinach 163
  Penne with sausage, fennel & garlic 158
  Quick jambalaya 185
  Risotto with sausage & red wine 191
  Sausage pittas with caramelised onions 19
  Tomato, sausage & Emmental croissants 26
  see also chorizo
seafood see clams; crab; mussels; squid
Smart beans on toast 22
sole, Dover
  Pan-fried fish fillets with crispy bacon 144
sole, lemon
  Fish & chips with herby dip 119
  Grilled flat fish with herb & caper dressing 143
  Pan-fried fish fillets with crispy bacon 144
soups
  Chilled avocado soup with zingy salsa 33
  Pea, lettuce & tarragon soup 29
  Summery Spanish-style soup 39
  Tuscan bean soup with rosemary & pesto 30
Spinach & chickpea curry 213
squid
  Chilli squid salad with peanuts 108
steak see under beef
stir-fries
  Honeyed duck & vegetable stir-fry 102
  Stir-fried kale with beef & black bean sauce 62
  Stir-fried tofu with summer vegetables 214

strawberries
  Chocolate-coated strawberries 266
  Strawberry & passion fruit salad 256
Summery Spanish-style soup 39
Sweet-and-sour prawns with lime 111
Sweet potato & goats' cheese frittata 240

T
Thai-poached salmon 136
Thai-style crab rice noodles 200
Tiramisu 262
Toffee banana trifles 269
Toffee sauce 281
Tofu with summer vegetables, Stir-fried 214
tomatoes
  Linguine with a fresh tomato & olive sauce 167
  Mushroom, tomato & egg burger 243
  Tomato & goats' cheese tarts 37
  Tomato, sausage & Emmental croissants 26
Tortellini with lemon & courgette 177
trifles 257, 269
Tuscan bean soup with rosemary & pesto 30

V
vegetables, mixed
  Roast vegetable, goats' cheese & lentil salad 242
  Stir-fried tofu with summer vegetables 214
  Summery Spanish-style soup 39
  Vegetable bolognese 221

W
Watercress, red onion & rosemary frittata 235

Y
yogurt
  Apple & ginger yogurt pots 274
  Low-fat yogurt & apricot pots 253